FOREVER WILD, FOREVER HOME

The Story of The Wild Animal Sanctuary of Colorado

FOREVER WILD, FOREVER HOME

The Story of The Wild Animal Sanctuary of Colorado

Pyree Square
Publishing

Forever Wild, Forever Home: The Story of The Wild Animal Sanctuary of Colorado

Published by Pyree Square Publishing LLC

Library of Congress Control Number: 2020946855

ISBN (hardcover): 9781662903199
ISBN (paperback): 9781662903205
eISBN: 9781662903212

Front cover: tiger "Simon"

Back cover clockwise from upper left: wolf "Olivia"; African lion "Jupiter" and his pride in the snow; black leopard "Eddy"; and grizzly bears "Natasha" and "Tiny"

For the tens of thousands of captive wild animals
who have yet to be rescued and given new homes

Contents

Acknowledgments

Forever Wild, Forever Home is the result of roughly eighteen months spent researching the captive wildlife crisis and volunteering, absorbing, and participating in the life and operations of The Wild Animal Sanctuary in Keenesburg, Colorado. It would not have been possible without the generous time commitment and ongoing support of Pat Craig and the Sanctuary team. Pat is the consummate storyteller whose indisputable expertise and highly entertaining insights into caring for hundreds of large carnivores drove this project and underscored its relevance in combating the captive wildlife crisis. Our heartfelt thanks to Pat for allowing us to include the more than 100 archival photos that bring the story of the Sanctuary to life.

We are indebted to all the staff at the Sanctuary and especially to Casey Craig for sharing his lifelong experience at the Sanctuary; Monica Craig for her enthusiastic support and for sifting through thousands of photos for the book; Becca Miceli for her wonderful tours of the habitats and the clinic, and her insights into the subtleties of caregiving for exotic animals; Kent Drotar for imparting his encyclopedic knowledge of the history and residents of the Sanctuary; Ryan Clements for his dedication and delightful stories; veterinarians Dr. Felicia Knightly and Dr. Joyce Thompson whose boundless dedication to captive wildlife health and welfare is inspiring and admirable; and Abby Matzke for all the work she does keeping us volunteers on the go and in the loop. We thank you all for your patience and kindness in continually fielding our questions and allowing us to become part of the Sanctuary.

We would like to thank all the volunteers at the Sanctuary for their dedication and hard work with a special thanks to: Jim Anderson, Jody Golden, Chris Humphreys, Jill Johnson, Nadine, Dee Pierce, Linda Selkurt, Joe Spahn, Grant and Nancy Steffen, Cynthia Streed, Kathy Weigle, and Nancy Williams for meeting with us and sharing their Sanctuary experiences. A special thanks to Chris Humphreys for her dedication to the Sanctuary and her wonderful photographs of its wild residents, many of which are contained in these pages.

We would also like to thank journalist Sharon Guynup and photographer Steve Winter whose work with *National Geographic* on tigers in the wild and captive big cats has been a ground-breaking and invaluable source of contextual information on the captive wildlife crisis; Brittany Peet, Deputy General Counsel for Captive Animal Law Enforcement with the PETA Foundation for her unceasing pursuit of animal welfare abusers and for helping us to better appreciate the keen intelligence and sensitivity of bears; and Dr. Peter Emily, Susanne Pilla, and the dentists who work with the Peter Emily International Veterinary Dental Foundation whose generosity and work around the world relieves pain and suffering that most of us could not tolerate. Our sincere appreciation goes to Rob Price, Kelly Santaguida, and the team at Gatekeeper Press for helping us bring *Forever Wild, Forever Home* to fruition.

Photo Acknowledgments

All photos are courtesy of The Wild Animal Sanctuary except the following, which are courtesy of:

John Eisele – 13.8
People for the Ethical Treatment of Animals – 3.3, 3.12, 3.13, 3.14, 7.2
The authors – 13.2, 13.5, 13.6, 14.2

"Saving one animal may not change the world,

but surely, for that one animal, the world will change forever!"

The Wild Animal Sanctuary's motto

Preface

:.: :.: :.: :.: :.: :.: :.: :.: :.: :.: :.: :.: :.: :.: :.: :.:
:.: :.: :.: :.: :.: :.: :.: :.: :.: :.: :.: :.: :.: :.: :.: :.:

Where Hope Begins

The Wild Animal Sanctuary is the leading large carnivore sanctuary in the world with more than 200 bears, nearly 170 big cats, and over 130 wolves and other exotic animals. For four decades, the Sanctuary has been rescuing animals from exotic wildlife trafficking rings, lion and tiger breeding mills, concrete bear pits, cub petting and selfie photo outfits, and suburban backyards. Many rescued animals have suffered from years or even decades of abuse. Roughly eighty-five percent have been law enforcement confiscations. Close to 200 have been rescued from other countries, yet there remain thousands of large carnivores in private hands and commercial businesses who continue to suffer cruelly.

The wild animals lucky enough to be rescued by the Sanctuary enjoy comfort and security, perhaps the first they have ever known. An innovative rehabilitation process works its magic on physical and psychological scars. Many animals see others of their own kind for the first time. They experience their first taste of freedom when they are released into enormous habitats carved out of thousands of acres of prairie and canyonlands.

The Wild Animal Sanctuary is often seen as the last hope for the animals who are rescued and brought here to their forever home. But those who visit, support, volunteer, and work here know that this is the place where hope begins.

We decided to write this book to share the story of The Wild Animal Sanctuary. The majority of the proceeds from book sales will go to the Sanctuary and its remarkable operations, ongoing expansion, and exciting future. We wish to honor the sanctity, nobility, and well-being of the animals who live here and the heroic and gratifying labors of those who care for them.

This is *their* story.

Melanie and Mark Shellenbarger

Chapter 1

A Place Like Nowhere Else

A s these pages come to life in the spring of 2020, we find ourselves sequestered in our Denver home under a stay-at-home mandate designed to combat the coronavirus pandemic. The world is in a state of voluntary paralysis because of COVID-19. People are social distancing and self-isolating, working from home, schooling from home, and entertaining themselves at home with games, social media, Zoom cocktail parties, and television binge-watching. *Tiger King: Murder, Mayhem and Madness*, the reality series that unmasked the bizarre world of big cat private ownership and the tiger trade in the United States, is the number one rated show on Netflix. The irony is not lost on us. More than sixty million viewers are spellbound by a TV show about tigers kept in cages while they themselves are confined to their homes. The difference, of course, is that we are staying home to try to avoid a crisis; captive wild animals are already in crisis.

We will forever remember the moment we first heard the words "captive wildlife crisis" on a perfectly ordinary Tuesday morning in April, during our inaugural visit to The Wild Animal Sanctuary outside of Keenesburg, Colorado. We had heard about the Sanctuary and vaguely remembered stories about Bolivian lion rescues, but we weren't even sure what a Bolivian lion was. We didn't really know what to expect and figured it might be like a zoo or a safari park where we would see some tigers, lions, or other wild animals and then drive back to our home in Denver. Little did we know that within a year, captive wild animals – and especially big cats and bears – would become a fixation for us, as we read, researched, and came to know intimately the scale and the scandal of the problem.

As we clipped along the highways north of Denver, the landscape around us grew increasingly rural. We shed the congestion of the city, the clutter of industrial warehouses that pepper the outskirts of the urban corridor, and then the last of the sprawling suburbs. As we neared The Wild

Animal Sanctuary, our drive took us down long and lonely country roads alongside barren fields bearing the rag-tag remnants of long-harvested wheat and sunflower crops, slumbering in wait for the spring sowing. Entering the large and airy Welcome Center and watching an introductory video play on an enormous screen, we learned that the Sanctuary is not a zoo at all. It is a not-for-profit global rescue operation that offers a unique rehabilitation process, large-acreage habitats, and a forever home for captive wild animals who have suffered inhumanely in cages or small chain link pens, many for decades, as part of entertainment schemes or as exotic pets in backyards and basements.

Tigers in backyards? How is it even possible, we wondered, to keep a lion or tiger as a pet? Are there really people out there who think it is cool to own a lion? Aren't there laws against this sort of thing? In fact, there are no federal laws that expressly prohibit ownership of big cats or bears, and hundreds of different state and local laws are only casually enforced or completely ignored. The cost of obtaining a license for a tiger is about the same as a license for your pet dog. We were stunned to learn that there are an estimated 5,000 to 10,000 tigers in private homes and commercial businesses in the United States, more than live in the wild in the rest of the world. Another 10,000 to 15,000 or more African lions, jaguars, leopards, black bears, grizzly bears, and other wild carnivores suffer the same fate. The Sanctuary's more than 500 residents represent a fraction of these captive big cats and bears. Then it hit us: the wild animals we were going to see have *never* been free. They were born in captivity and raised in captivity. Unlike their unlucky brethren who will die or be killed while living under often horrific conditions, the rescued animals at the Sanctuary will live out their natural lives in safety and comfort.

That fine April morning, climbing a broad stairway to an elevated walkway under a crystal blue sky we beheld an endless prairie landscape with enormous wildlife habitats reaching to the horizon. Returning to the Sanctuary season after season, we have seen rail-thin, dull-eyed, newly-rescued animals transformed over months into magnificent creatures with glossy coats, powerful muscles, and shining eyes. We have been enraptured by African lions bounding through grassy meadows, sleek tigers sliding through snow, and great bears basking under brilliantly blue skies. We have never tired of seeing a giant Kodiak bear rising slowly from a deep pool hidden by lush prairie grass; a lion turning its nose into the wind, his dark and tawny mane ruffling in the breeze; and a jaguar leaping effortlessly onto a lofty log perch. We continue to be stopped in our tracks by the howling of wolves and barking of hyenas. We have heard tigers chuff in greeting, mountain lions purr with joy, and African lions roar in winter.

The Wild Animal Sanctuary changed our lives, as it has for so many others who visit, volunteer, and work here. Over the past eighteen months, we have delved into cub trafficking rings and tiger mills that churn out untold litters every year – and learned about captive big cat tourism long before *Tiger King* became all the rage. We have absorbed disturbing accounts of pay-to-play cub petting venues, photo operations, and even pay-to-swim schemes in which frightened tiger and lion cubs, torn from their mothers when only days or weeks old, are hustled from visitor to visitor. Tales of white tigers have transported us into the jungles of India and shuttered circuses have taken us to the dense forests of Bolivia. Lions in Ohio backyards, bears in Maryland corn cribs, and wolves in Iowa shopping malls have acquainted us with labyrinthine laws that fail to protect wild animals from people and people from wild animals. Neglect and abuse of big cats and bears has introduced us to roadside zoos and bear pits, where animals are often caged and mistreated for years on end. Follow the money, we learned, and it will lead you to a global multi-billion dollar exotic animal trafficking enterprise, third in magnitude behind illegal drugs and weapons.

Animal trafficking is driven by profiteers exploiting the vast amounts of money to be made in prolifically breeding, selling, and exhibiting tigers, lions, and other exotic animals. These self-styled conservationists operate unsavory, and in many cases illegal, enterprises while posing as bastions of large carnivore preservation, which they are not. *Tiger King* focuses on "Joe Exotic," the owner of an Oklahoma roadside zoo and a key player in the U.S. exotic animal trafficking arena. He ran one of the largest tiger breeding operations in the U.S., bragging that he owned more than 200 tigers among his more than 1,000 animals.

But *Tiger King*, you see, misses a key point. The sensationalist miniseries casts the big cats themselves – pacing in fetid and barren cages; engaged in a feeding frenzy; and bred again and again to feed the coffers of their exploiters – in a supporting role. It never explores their mistreatment or covers The Wild Animal Sanctuary's rescue of thirty-nine tigers and three bears from Joe Exotic's Wynnewood, Oklahoma zoo in the fall of 2017. In fact, the Sanctuary has been rescuing captive animals from the Joe Exotics of the world for forty years.

Tiger King never told you about the rescues, but we will. That is where our story begins.

One Rescue at a Time

When we first meet Pat Craig, founder and Director of The Wild Animal Sanctuary, and Kent Drotar, its Public Relations Director, to discuss our idea for this book we are a little nervous. Whether they will warm to the idea is anybody's guess, and we need their support and assistance if the project is going to work. Kent greets us at the Welcome Center entrance. He is a tall and striking man with a pleasant and approachable manner. Having started as a Sanctuary volunteer in 2009, Kent has an encyclopedic knowledge of the history of the Sanctuary and can portray in lively and entertaining detail the story of each of the hundreds of animals who live here. We will later learn that Kent periodically gives personal tours for small groups of volunteers to bring them up to date on what is happening at the Sanctuary; the online sign-up sheet fills up in a flash.

We follow Kent through the Welcome Center and take a table in the Lion's Den Café to await Pat's arrival. A curious and unusual entourage suddenly appears. Pat walks slowly across the great hall with five enormous Irish Wolfhounds in tow. The hounds stride immediately behind him. A stout English Bulldog paddles along behind. Not surprisingly, given the heft and commanding appearance of his greater brethren, we notice a fuzzy, tiny Maltese only later.

Wearing the Sanctuary's brilliant-orange signature hoodie and slouchy faded blue jeans, Pat enters the Lion's Den with this incongruous pack. We are immediately surrounded by roughly 1,000 pounds of pooches with curious, fuzzy faces and coarse oily coats. Dog lovers that we are – and especially *big* dog lovers – we are thrilled. The largest male, Floyd, weighs 250 pounds. Lizzy paws at Melanie's arm for attention. Betty leans into Mark for a hug. Matilda, the largest of the girls, lays her head in Kent's lap. Butchie, the bulldog, snuffles about searching for tidbits that have fallen to the floor. Marcel, the Maltese, plays with a plastic bottle cap. After the meet and greet, each of the dogs claims a space around the table and sinks to the floor, content to snooze while their pack leader conducts his meeting.

The two colleagues, who have worked together for more than a decade, briefly review the history of the Sanctuary and the move to the present location near Keenesburg in 1994. Over the years, the Sanctuary has grown to 789 acres and is home to not only bears, African lions, and tigers, but also jaguars, leopards, mountain lions, wolves, coyotes, bobcats, lynx, foxes, and an assortment of other exotic carnivores and hoofed stock. All have been rescued. Pat and Kent tell us stories about the solitary nature of

1.1 Pat Craig and his dog pack

tigers, the convivial disposition of African lions, the peripatetic curiosity of bears – and the keen intelligence of all these species.

Pat describes the red tape and bureaucratic tangles the Sanctuary navigates endlessly to rescue captive animals, not only from across the United States, but around the world as well. He has rescued nearly 200 animals from other countries, including Mexico, Argentina, Spain, South Korea, and a tiny island in the Pacific called Saipan. Both domestic and international rescues continue apace, and the frequency and magnitude of the rescues are increasing as the captive wildlife crisis grows. We are again stunned and chagrined by our ignorance of this problem.

We learn about the Sanctuary's tripartite mission to rescue wild animals; rehabilitate and care for them over their natural lifetimes; and educate the public about the causes of and solutions to the captive wildlife crisis. Public education, they say, may be the best hope for arresting and perhaps, someday, ending the problem. To that end, the Sanctuary opened to the public in 2002 and since then the educational mission has grown astronomically with the construction of a new, enormous Welcome Center and the completion of the Mile into the Wild Walkway, an elevated footbridge that literally provides visitors with a bird's eye view of the Sanctuary's residents.

The men praise the hard working and dedicated staff and the army of volunteers, without whom the Sanctuary would not be possible. The Wolfhounds and other dogs are rescues too, and since everyone at the Sanctuary plays an important role, even they step in when needed as caretakers for young lion and tiger cubs who have been separated from their mothers.

Habitat acreage has been fully built out at the Sanctuary; there is no room for more animals here. So, fully committed to continue tackling the captive wildlife crisis, the Sanctuary recently purchased land at a second site. Pat and Kent's enthusiasm for The Wild Animal Refuge, the Sanctuary's newest and to-date most ambitious project, is evident. Covering 9,684 acres of rock outcroppings, grassy meadows, and deep ravines, this new haven in the remote canyonlands of southeastern Colorado accepted its first rescues in 2019 and will ultimately grow to more than a thousand residents.

Pat is humble and pleasant in demeanor, unassuming yet quietly self-confident as he talks about the Sanctuary, the Refuge, and his life's work. He wears a mantle of undeterred resolve worn by the rigors of constant fundraising (the Sanctuary is a not-for-profit organization that exists solely on donations and, unlike public zoos, receives no government monies); worry about his hundreds of beloved carnivores; despair at the suffering he sees constantly; and a sense of enormous gratification knowing that the Sanctuary has been working for almost four decades to alleviate that suffering.

We present our book idea. Our intent is to help educate people about the captive wildlife crisis by sharing the story of The Wild Animal Sanctuary. We want to convey the stories of the animals who live here but also celebrate the staff and volunteers who care for them and the remarkable place they call home. Our plan is to observe and participate in the life of the Sanctuary over the course of a year. To gain an appreciation for its operations, we will sign up as volunteers ourselves, which we had planned to do in any case. At first concerned that Pat and Kent will not give us the go-ahead to proceed with the project, we quickly grasp that they are all for it – provided we do not consume too much precious time of their staff and volunteers.

Pat is content to let us give this book a try; if it fails, he will try something else, if it succeeds, all the better. We get the impression that if we told him we wanted to start a chicken farm to help feed his big cats, he would have smiled and said, "Go for it!" Indeed, when we later learn how much food it takes to satisfy the voracious appetites of his more than 500 residents (roughly 70,000 pounds *per week*), we realize the chicken farm idea most definitely has merit.

At the close of our meeting, Pat stands up and the Wolfhounds rise one by one. Pat opens the door of the café and the dog pack files out. He saunters down the hall and again the five giants move into position behind him, with Butchie bringing up the rear (Miniature Marcel is, once again, lost to view among the massive hounds). None of the dogs wear collars. None are on leashes. Pat gives no commands. This is a display of complete off-leash control that would be the envy of any obedience or agility trial competitor. Yet, we realize, it is not about control; it is about connection and companionship, loyalty, and leadership. These giants of the dog world and their more diminutive companions simply follow Pat because they want to do so. As the year elapses, it will become clear that where Pat goes, so goes the Sanctuary dog family.

It has been a rewarding sixty minutes with Pat Craig and Kent Drotar, a remarkable visit to an extraordinary place. Over the next year we will come to know and gain a tremendous amount of respect for the other members of Pat's core team, drawn mostly from the Sanctuary's volunteer corps: Casey Craig, Chief Operating Officer; Becca Miceli, Chief Science and Welfare Officer; Ryan Clements, Director of Operations, Monica Craig, Communications Director; Dr. Joyce Thompson, veterinarian; Dr. Felicia Knightly, consulting veterinarian; and Abby Matzke, Volunteer Coordinator – and all of the staff and volunteers who embody a passion, energy, and commitment to the Sanctuary that would be the envy of any organization anywhere.

We cannot believe how much we have absorbed about The Wild Animal Sanctuary and its exceptional founder, and the story of its mission to end the captive wildlife crisis. As the year goes on and we learn more of the horrors of captive wildlife, hear astounding stories of courageous rescues, and begin to understand the sacrifices made by the Sanctuary team and other wild animal advocates around the world, we come to appreciate that in this first encounter, we have but scratched the surface.

In truth, at this point we know hardly any of it. We do not realize that forty years ago Pat Craig not only rescued his first jaguar, but also took the first bold steps on a journey that would forever change the captive wildlife paradigm – one rescue at a time.

Chapter 2

꓾ ꓾ ꓾ ꓾ ꓾ ꓾ ꓾ ꓾ ꓾ ꓾ ꓾ ꓾ ꓾ ꓾ ꓾ ꓾ ꓾

It's a Himalayan!

With its prairie location, vast acreage, considerable complement of large carnivores, remarkable tenure of forty years, and massive new expansion at The Wild Animal Refuge, The Wild Animal Sanctuary is unique among exotic animal rescue and refuge operations. Yet, as Kent Drotar remarked to us, "Pat Craig never set out to start a large animal sanctuary." So, how did this completely unexpected journey begin?

The story of The Wild Animal Sanctuary begins not in Keenesburg, but four decades ago in 1980, when the captive wildlife crisis was in its infancy. Wild animal acts flourished at Ringling Bros. and Barnum & Bailey Circus and other similar venues. Wild animal use in film and television drew viewers in droves to watch Clarence the Cross-Eyed Lion, the dolphin Flipper, and black bear Gentle Ben. Tourists driving I-95 south might stop to visit a bear pit, where they could (weirdly) peer down into deep concrete bunkers at the pit's unlucky inhabitants and whose unlucky inhabitants could stare (longingly) up at them. Roadside zoos that exhibited lions and tigers in tiny cages were increasing in number. Public zoos were breeding an increasing number of animals to provide a steady supply of the adorable babies that brought visitors in the doors. And what happened when the baby animals grew up? That is the dark side of the enterprise that few people know about and no one wants to think about. Those animals became part of what zoos euphemistically label their "surplus" inventory.

During a back-of-the-house tour at a zoo in early 1979, Pat Craig got his first shocking look at this "surplus" animal problem. A University of Colorado freshman driving back to Boulder from Christmas break in Florida, he took a detour to briefly visit a friend in North Carolina, planning to then "book it" home to Denver in time for the start of spring semester. The friend happened to be a groundskeeper at a local city zoo

---

and offered Pat a tour of the premises. Covering both front-of-the-house and behind-the-scenes operations, the tour proved to be a fascinating glimpse into zoo life, up until the point when they wandered into a warehouse area beyond the fringes of the tourist realm. The warehouse and its immediate surroundings served as a holding area where the zoo kept the wild animals for which they had no room in "front-of-the-house" habitats. Pat, stunned and sickened by what he saw, still cringes at the vivid and appalling memory of this wild animal storehouse:

I found dozens of "surplus" animals such as lions, tigers, leopards and other formerly majestic creatures being kept in tiny cramped cages – bathed only in artificial light and stacked in neat little lines like cans of old forgotten food in some dusty pantry...They were such small cages like dog runs about 4 feet wide by 8 to 10 feet long. You couldn't keep more than one animal in each cage. It was just enough that they could come up, turn around, and pace back, come up, turn around, and pace back. It stunk and there wasn't much light...I thought, 'You should be able to solve this.' I asked if they take turns with the animals on view and he said 'no.' I said, 'Geez, are they going to live here their whole life?' He said, 'No, we try to get them to go somewhere else or we euthanize them.'

For Pat, the most heartbreaking part of the enterprise was that these were healthy animals. They were not sick, diseased, or nearing the end of their natural lives. Disgusted by the experience, Pat returned home to Boulder, back to classes and running the family gas station, but he could not stop thinking about what he had seen. Something needed to be done. But what? And by whom?

So what was it that fueled my desire to actually step in and help these animals? Was it the inhumane living conditions...or possibly the look they had in their eyes as I passed by them one after another? Or could it have been the sickness that I felt knowing that these regal animals were not only permanently confined within this hidden dungeon – but also most of them either die from the caustic effects of a broken spirit...or will be killed in order to make room for the ever-growing number of cast-off creatures. It was all that, and so much more! How could I feel good about myself knowing that there had probably been hundreds of people who had witnessed what I had, yet none of them had ever done anything about it? Over and over again, one human after another had come and gone only to shake their heads in silence or move on mumbling something like 'Somebody ought to do something about this.'

Fortunately, somebody did. Over the next year, Pat would lay the groundwork for what would ultimately become the largest captive wild carnivore sanctuary in the world. He would send letters to zoological and wild animal facilities across the country asking if they were looking for homes for their surplus animals. Shockingly, he would receive dozens of replies in response to his queries. The replies had one thing in common, a single resounding answer: YES!

The Journey Begins: Boulder Zoological Inc.

Pat grew up on a fifteen-acre family farm along Valmont Road outside the town of Boulder, Colorado. Although his father had businesses in Boulder, his parents had grown up on farms in Kansas and Nebraska and wanted their children to experience some measure of country life. More of a gentleman's farm than a working farm, the family kept chickens, a couple of horses, a cow, pigs, and they grew a bit of corn and vegetables. Pat figured there was certainly enough room for a few lions and tigers as well.

In the pre-internet and pre-laptop days of the late 1970s, the letter writing enterprise involved a mechanical typewriter from Pat's grandmother, a list of every licensed zoo in the country, and a lot of whiteout to correct the profusion of mistakes typical of typing endeavors at the time. But before he even keyed a stroke, Pat requested the necessary zoning change and applied for U.S. Department of Agriculture (USDA) and Colorado Division of Wildlife licenses. He then built the requisite enclosures and had them inspected and approved by the licensing authorities. After incorporating as Boulder Zoological Inc. – the name inspired by the fact that he lived in Boulder County and "everybody else" at the time had "zoological" in their company name – the only thing left to do was bring some wild carnivores on board. To that end and upon receipt of his federal and state licenses, Pat started typing, signing, and mailing about ten or fifteen letters a day.

Boulder Zoological Inc. was in business and the zoos across the country were lining up to become its first customer. Within a couple of weeks, Pat's mailbox was flooded with replies. "Every list," he remembers, "had multiple animals." There were elephants (elephants!), chimpanzees, an alligator, giraffes, zebras, and bears, but most of the animals on the list were big cats. Pat also learned about the curious notation system zoos use for their animal inventories. The lists would state, for example, "African Lions, 1.2," which begs the question, what is .2 of an African Lion? "I was completely naïve," Pat says sheepishly, "I had no idea...so the first one I talked to, I said, oh by the way, it says 1.2 and they said, yeah, that means we have one male and two females." He smiles, "It was a lot more forgiving environment back then."

Facing an overwhelming response to his query letters, and just beginning to appreciate the magnitude of the problem, Pat was beginning to wonder what he might be getting himself into. By virtue of a casual visit on the way home from a college break at Christmas, he had inadvertently wandered into a world he never knew existed and which he knew little about. The whole absurdity of the wild animal surplus problem seemed beyond belief, like stepping into C.S. Lewis's wardrobe and finding yourself in Narnia or sliding down Lewis Carroll's rabbit hole with Alice in Wonderland. In fact, Pat was beginning to doubt the feasibility of his own "zoological" enterprise, recalling, "All of a sudden, I started thinking about it and wasn't sure if I was really going to be able to help."

Freckles Flies to Denver

In looking back on our conversations with Pat about the beginnings of The Wild Animal Sanctuary and delving into its history, it seems to us that over the course of a few short years, Pat made two momentous wild animal rescue decisions. Those decisions would forever change the course of his life and set the future trajectory of large carnivore sanctuaries across the United States. The first was Freckles. The second was Platteville.

In 1979, Pat was letting the letters pile up from the zoos while he tried to figure out what to do next. Writing to the zoos and other animal facilities was one thing. Acquiring his first large (or in truth, not so large) carnivore was quite another.

"Next" materialized in the form of a young woman sobbing on the other end of the phone in early January 1980. Pat's mother, who was beginning to grasp the seriousness of her son's exotic animal rehoming ambitions, delivered the phone message after Pat got home from class that evening. The sobbing young woman was with a zoo that had received Pat's surplus animal letter and asked that Pat call her back. When they connected by phone the next day, she introduced herself as an intern at a small zoo in North Carolina (with no affiliation to the zoo Pat had previously visited), who had been given the responsibility to take care of three baby jaguars. The cubs had just been born and had been rejected by their mother. Two had already died from pneumonia and, she started crying again, "I don't want to kill the last one." Pat asked what the zoo staff and veterinarians were doing to help. She admitted that the zoo did not have a full time vet and there were only two paid staff members; all the other positions were filled by volunteers like herself. As an aside, at the time even large city zoos often did not have full time veterinarians. There was little preventive care; when an animal got sick and died, the zoo replaced it.

The jaguar situation presented quite a conundrum. Pat had built enclosures for large carnivores, not for a week-old baby jaguar. He could not put a baby out there, especially in the middle of a Colorado winter! Plus, he'd never thought about rescuing cubs; his plan was to rescue the kinds of animals he had seen with his friend on the back-of-the-house tour earlier that year – full grown, in the prime of life, unneeded and unwanted, and eventually destined to be euthanized. But now this call had come in. The question was, what to do about it? Pat puzzled the problem out with his friends. The jaguar cub was a *wild* cat, just not a *big wild* cat. He had done a tremendous amount of work over the past year. The animal was clearly in distress. What, he thought, and his friends concurred, did he have to lose?

What indeed? In what would be the first momentous decision of the sanctuary enterprise that would become his life's work, Pat booked a flight. To say his plans were not fully developed at that point would be rather an understatement. To say he was winging it would be spot on. A follow up call to the airline before he ever left Denver – but after he had booked the flight – confirmed his worst suspicions. Yes, he could carry a small animal on the plane. No, he could not take a jaguar on the plane. Pat explained to the airline official, "It's only five or ten days old. It can't hurt anybody." "No," the voice firmly stated on the other end of the line, "you cannot take a jaguar on the plane." Pat went to North Carolina anyway, figuring "I'd already bought the ticket so I may as well go," and perhaps imagining in the back of his mind that he wasn't really going to come home with a baby jaguar, was he? Reflecting about the airline problem, he admits, "I didn't know how I was going to solve it," and about the baby jaguar, he concedes, "I kind of thought it might be dead when I got there."

We are relatively sure that most of us can remember our first flight, where we were going, and the occasion for the trip. If you were too young to remember your first flight, your parents likely have regaled you with the details of this modern rite of passage. Regardless of the time, place, and occasion, however, we would bet a lot of money that none of us flew 1,500 miles cross-country to collect a baby jaguar. Yet that was the occasion for Pat's first-ever flight. Disembarking in North Carolina without even an animal carrier, he arrived at the zoo in a taxi and had the driver wait. The intern brought the weak and suffering baby cub out, thrust her and a bottle of milk in Pat's arms, found a small clamshell cat carrier to house the cub during the flight, thanked him, and wished him well. Pat was stunned, thinking "You're really going to let me walk out of here with a baby jaguar?" No license. No transfer papers. No vet records. Just a baby jaguar in a clamshell cat carrier. It was a dramatic introduction to the dearth of wild animal ownership laws in this country and to the ease with which such animals changed hands back then – and now.

Pat examined his new charge. A full grown golden jaguar is covered with ebony rosettes from head to tail, a stunningly beautiful dappling that affords the animal outstanding camouflage in jungle habitats. The nameless, distressed cub in Pat's arms had a "zillion little spots," which was the reason he later christened her "Freckles." A full grown female jaguar can weigh as much as two hundred pounds; Freckles weighed less than two pounds. A full grown female jaguar might be five or six feet from the nose to the base of the tail; Freckles measured less than twelve inches. Except for the fact that she had round ears rather than the pointed ears of a housecat, Pat says, "You might think it was a baby kitten, just kind of a *sturdy* looking one!" The future was, literally, in Pat's hands and sturdy was an understatement. Even at a little more than a week old and close to death, Freckle's robust build already hinted at the massive limbs and great strength of the jaguar – the big cat with a bite force that pound for pound exceeds any other – that she would ultimately become.

Thankfully, however "sturdy" she was, Freckles fit neatly in the cat carrier and Pat whisked her into the taxi and off to the airport. Pat never expected to rescue a baby animal and never imagined he would really walk out of the zoo with a baby jaguar in a cat carrier, and now he had Freckles. He also never expected to have to figure out how to fly back with an animal to which the airline had already denied passage. Yet, off to the airport they went with Pat thinking, "What am I going to do? They are going to tell me no. I'm going to have to catch a train to get back to Colorado." In the pre-security days of the 1980s, Pat progressed easily through the airport terminal on his way to the gate with his clamshell cub. He recalls, "I remember walking to get on the plane and I'm sweating it and sweating it. And I'm carrying this little clamshell thing." As he stepped through the passenger door and onto the flight, his worst fears were realized when the stewardess said brightly, "'Oh, what do you have?' I said, 'It's a kitten.' 'Oh,' she replied, 'Let me see.' So I opened it up and she said, 'It's really cute but...what *kind* of a kitten is this?' She could see it had round ears and it was...*sturdier.* I replied, 'Oh, it's a Himalayan!'"

Into the Future of Exotic Animal Rescue

So it began. Pat's first momentous decision in the fight for captive wildlife was acquiring a tiny baby jaguar named Freckles. He stayed home for a week from school, nursing his tiny "Himalayan," afraid to leave her for any length of time lest she die.

Freckles became stronger and stronger, began moving around, and started to suck on the bottle. "The next six months," says Pat, "was a giant learning curve. Once she was mobile, she was like a little Tasmanian Devil with little tiny claws that were bigger than a full-grown housecat's. She was incredibly smart and that was my biggest challenge...She would pick up on behaviors and patterns, it really blew my mind." Freckles, who was barely alive when Pat held her for the first time, grew up to be smart, savvy, and gorgeous. She would live for twenty-four years and become the "first lady" of The Wild Animal Sanctuary.

2.1 Baby Freckles

2.2 Freckles

In 1980, however, Pat was just getting comfortable with Freckles, trying to stay one step ahead of her, feed her and care for her, and learn how to move her from one enclosure to another. Meanwhile, the calls and letters from zoos kept coming. Plus, the word was getting out to other wild animal venues. "One by one," he remembers, "they started calling. The people who were calling me were always the ones that had run out of options." Pat agreed to take in a female mountain lion from a Farmington, Utah amusement park. The park said they had gotten rid of other animals and planned to put her down if they were unable to find another facility to take her. Pat named the mountain lion Scruffy "because she didn't come with a name...She was 'mountain lion number something or other.'" Then he took in a black bear named Fozzie from Lion Country Safari in Irvine, California. He met a guy on a road somewhere between the state of Washington and Colorado to pick up an African lion cub named Leo.

Pat's perfunctory meeting with Leo's owner only corroborated the latter's cluelessness. "He pulls up in a U-Haul," Pat recalls, "He goes in the back and rolls up the hatch and there's this little lion cub just sitting there, bouncing around on the road the whole time...He goes, 'Here he is!' He scoops him up and turns around, hands him to me, and says, 'I gotta go because I've got to get back to work. See ya!'" It was only then that Pat realized he had a sick lion cub on his hands. He remembers, "I had a pickup truck with a cage in the back, but I didn't put him in it because he was so weak. So I put him in the cab, and he rode back with me the whole way in the cab."

Leo, who could barely walk, was suffering from a crippling disability called Metabolic Bone Disease (MBD). Leo's inexperienced and frantic owner, who could not get rid of the cub fast enough, and his inexperienced and incompetent veterinarian, "had him on milk up to eight weeks. Then his vet said 'you can wean him like a puppy.' He was actually giving him dog food, and no calcium, so his bones were like rubber and he was sick because he wasn't getting any nutrition." Calcium is a critical mineral for lion health. Quite simply, if overall blood calcium levels are low, the felid body will leach calcium from the bones to redirect the mineral toward the maintenance of critical bodily functions. MBD results in incredibly weak, even soft bones. In the early stages, a young cat may show signs of lameness or bowed front legs. As the disease advances, the lion – like Leo – may be unable to stand or walk, suffer a variety of fractures, and exhibit stunted growth, misshapen limbs and neurological problems that can result in death. Wild lions meet their calcium requirements by eating the whole carcass, stripping meat, and grinding up the bones of their prey. Captive lions must be given calcium supplements to maintain health and growth. Dog food will not cut it. Pat immediately got Leo on a proper diet with enough calcium and other nutrients. But for months he carried Leo outside to eat and to relieve himself until the cub's bones were strong enough to support his ever-increasing bulk. As a result of Pat's selfless dedication and Leo's tremendous trust in him, the great lion and the young man developed a special relationship that lasted for twenty-three years.

2.3 Pat Craig and Leo, his first lion rescue

At this point Pat had a jaguar, a mountain lion, a black bear, and an African lion. To learn about the care and feeding of four different species, he had garnered information from reading books, chatting with zookeepers, poring over regulations and laws, and simply observing and working with the animals themselves. Pat was clearly committed to saving captive wild animals, but what if he had said at the time, "This little jaguar has gotten way bigger, way faster than I was expecting. Oops, this lion is too much to handle! This bear is stronger than I ever anticipated. Things are getting a little dicey and dangerous." He could have conceded, "Well, I gave it my best shot. It was a worthwhile experiment. I love Freckles and my other animals, but geez, this is a lot of responsibility. I've worked my way up the learning curve of the animal welfare laws. I've spent countless hours figuring out how to feed and care for large carnivores, worrying about how to keep them healthy and where to find a vet when they need one, building cages and habitat fences that keep them (and everyone else) safe and yet give them the room they need to roam in order to be healthy and content. The captive wildlife problem is simply too big for me to solve. Besides, it's expensive to feed a jaguar, a mountain lion, a black bear, and an African lion! How am I going to make ends meet? And I cannot delegate their care to anyone else. Will I ever be able to take a vacation?"

What if Pat had asked himself these questions? What if Pat had decided to stop with Leo what he had started with Freckles? What if Pat had decided to abandon his captive wildlife avocation? There never would have been a Sanctuary now celebrating its fortieth anniversary.

That is what Pat could have said and could have done. Instead, he made a second momentous decision. Adopting Freckles was the crucial first step, but a decision in early 1982 to rescue thirteen abused big cats in the nearby town of Platteville would launch him on the treacherous and turbulent rollercoaster of captive wildlife rescue for the next four decades. What he found there was more vicious than he could ever have imagined.

Even today among well-established wildlife sanctuaries, the Platteville rescue would be considered a sizable, formidable, and horrific undertaking. It all started when Pat received a call from the American Humane Society in Denver about thirteen big cats being raised by a medical doctor on a Platteville farm. Thirteen big cats would quadruple his complement of large carnivores! Yet, when he learned the doctor was raising the animals to kill them for their pelts, Pat agreed to accept the rescues. He was twenty-two years old at the time. When the police, the American Humane Society, the veterinarian, and Pat met at the farm, "There was a long chicken coop… like a loafing shed with a slanted roof. There was a door at each end." Between the doors there was a long passageway with cages on both sides. The windows were closed. There were three light bulbs dangling from the ceiling, but only one worked. The team made their way into the darkness amidst the frightening sounds of big animals moving around and urine and feces flying when the cats flicked their tails. "The ammonia was so bad you couldn't even breathe…It was a dark dungeon. We opened the door at the other end to try to get some light and some air."

In the dim light from the open doors, the team could see the horror of it all. There were African lions, tigers, leopards, and jaguars who had, quite literally, been living in the dark for years. The animals had been confined to a one-story, windowless barn with no ventilation and an unforgiving concrete floor. There was "no drainage," Pat recalls, "just feces this deep [he holds his hands about six or eight inches apart] and urine. There were these wooden boxes the cats could get on to get out of all that crap. But there was no way to rinse it down or hose it down. There were no drains, just concrete all the way around." Imprisoned in small, chain link cages, the animals were mired in their own filth. Pat was stricken. Although the animals he had taken in so far might have been malnourished, they had been clean. But this was hideous. "This was sheer abuse...no windows, no natural light, no anything, just that one light bulb. It was just one giant shock."

There was no way to move the animals without sedating them. Pat brought the tranquilizer gun and the darts. The vet brought the drugs. One by one each animal went down. As the team carried the animals out into the sunshine, they could see claws that were tremendously overgrown, and teeth that were broken or had been filed down. Pat was revolted by inhumane treatment he had never before seen nor imagined. He remembers coming to the shocking realization that if he were to continue down this path, "This is what the future holds. People like this. Horrific places." He grimaces, "I've been to plenty since then."

The journey from Freckles to thirteen big cats in a dark prison of a barn was a sobering acknowledgment of the extent and gravity of the captive large carnivore problem. It would become clear that the issue encompassed not only surplus animals at publicly-supported zoos, but also large numbers of roadside exhibits, cub pay-to-play petting and photo-op venues, breeding and other for-profit businesses – not to mention private owners keeping big cats and bears as "pets." The remarkably uplifting story of the Sanctuary and its growth over the years underpins the tragic escalation of the trade in exotic animals. The problem – which would become known as the captive wildlife crisis – would grow astronomically over the next forty years.

Chapter 3

❖ ❖ ❖ ❖ ❖ ❖ ❖ ❖ ❖ ❖ ❖ ❖ ❖ ❖ ❖ ❖
❖ ❖ ❖ ❖ ❖ ❖ ❖ ❖ ❖ ❖ ❖ ❖ ❖ ❖ ❖ ❖

Confronting the Captive Wildlife Crisis

Media outlets were abuzz in early 2019 when police received an anonymous tip from a caller who had broken into an abandoned house in Houston looking for an inconspicuous place to smoke some weed. Thinking he had discovered an unassuming bolt-hole where he could get high in the privacy of someone else's home, the intruder found himself face to face with a very large tiger in a very small cage. The cage door was secured with a screwdriver and a flimsy nylon strap. The tiger had no access to water or food. The police followed up on the call, authorities stepped in, and the tiger was rescued to a new home at an animal sanctuary southeast of Dallas. The stoner's whereabouts are unreported.

While this tiger encounter may be entertaining, we believe it speaks to serious issues. Wild animal welfare and protection laws vary widely from state to state. Texas state law permits exotic animal ownership if the owner obtains a USDA license and a county permit, so the Houston tiger may well have been a legally owned "pet." Kind of like owning a poodle, right? Well, not really, because a respectably bred poodle will probably set you back considerably more money than a generic tiger. As hard as it is to believe, it can be less expensive to purchase an exotic carnivore than a purebred dog. Icon, a young male African lion rescued by The Wild Animal Sanctuary, was purchased by his Ohio owners for $450 at a local exotic wildlife auction.

In this case, the intruder was lucky but the tiger even luckier. The former may be bragging about his encounter at tailgate parties and family reunions for years to come. Even better he was not killed by a ravenous tiger who had broken out of his flimsy cage desperate for food and water. But to our way of thinking, the tiger won the day. His story could have been heartbreaking, as it is for so many caged wild animals, who suffer and die from dehydration or starvation. The tiger was released into a grassy five-acre habitat (quite possibly the first grass he had ever set foot on) at a Texas animal sanctuary where he will live out the rest of his long life.

As this story demonstrates, exotic "pets" are more common – and legal – than we might think. Little Bear, Cupcake, Buster, and Yogi were all acquired by separate owners across America who at some point realized that bears do not make good pets and surrendered them to the Sanctuary. African lion cub "Baby Leo" was a birthday present for a four-year old girl. Predictably, but sooner than anyone expected, Baby Leo got too rough to handle and the family dumped him at a derelict zoo where he was rescued by the Sanctuary. Today he is a young king lion with a pride of his own. Mountain lion Romeo was chained by the neck in a Montana backyard before he was rescued by the Sanctuary as a one-year old cub; he grew into a magnificent 170-pound cougar.

Today an estimated 15,000 to 25,000 or more captive big cats, bears, and other smaller carnivores such as bobcats, wolves, and foxes live as "pets" in private homes and serve as "props" for commercial enterprises in the U.S. Yet no one really knows the number of such carnivores in captivity, since there is no regulatory mechanism through which to track them. And lest anyone think the United States stands alone in perpetuating the captive wildlife crisis, large carnivores are owned as pets or used for commercial profit throughout the world. Another 5,000 or more tigers can be found in China where they live mostly on "tiger farms" and are bred to be slaughtered for food such as tiger bone soup (held to be a remedy for rheumatism) and for other "parts" which are considered essential to many "natural" Chinese medicines.

Consider this dilemma carefully because it foretells a bleak future: big cats in the wild are on their way to extinction while the number in captivity is increasing apace. Just one hundred years ago, there were as many as 100,000 wild tigers across Asia; today there are fewer than 4,000. The number of wild African lions, leopards, and jaguars has also been in freefall for the last fifty years and all three are listed as "endangered" by the Endangered Species Act (ESA). Wild African lions, for example, numbered 200,000 in Africa a century ago; there are only 20,000 left today. Bears have been somewhat more fortunate, although their numbers too are in decline. The famed grizzly bears of Yellowstone National Park, for example, are a threatened population.

The loss of apex and keystone predators – the carnivores at the top of the food chain and those who play a major role in maintaining the equilibrium of an ecosystem – can throw the self-regulating mechanisms of that biome into disarray. Habitat degradation, fragmentation, and destruction; rising human-animal conflict resulting from ever-increasing human population growth; and poaching are among the key reasons for what will be their tragic demise if the numbers cannot be reversed.

But please recognize, we are dealing with two distinct calamities. The rapid loss of large carnivores in the wild contrasts sharply with their dramatic increase in captivity. Species decline is highly publicized. The captive wildlife crisis is largely unknown. Could there be more irony to this situation? It seems inconceivable that, given the tragic scope of wild animal extinction around the globe, there should be an upsurge in wild animals held captive where they do not belong. But there is.

Why Own a Tiger...or a Lion...or any Exotic Animal?

While most of us would never consider purchasing a pet tiger, lion, bear, or other dangerous animal, a significant number of people do just that. Individuals may own an exotic animal for a variety of reasons: the status afforded the owner of an unusual animal; a desire to commune with the natural world through a wild animal surrogate; the power or machismo associated with controlling a dangerous creature; a misguided belief in one's power as an animal communicator who is telepathically in tune with animal idioms; or to live out a sort of codependent fantasy that their relationship with an exotic pet is mutually supportive and loving. We do not dispute that many people love their tigers and lions. The problem is they believe their tigers and lions love them back in the same way.

Some people relish exotic animal ownership so much they become collectors, or even hoarders, amassing more and more wild animals over time. Others move beyond pet ownership into commercial exhibiting, showmanship, or other entertainments to flaunt members of their menagerie, and to support the enormous expense of keeping them. The more ambitious, unscrupulous, and greedy among them might be drawn into the dark worlds of cub petting and cub photo ops, and the breeding and animal trafficking operations needed to sustain them.

Sadly, there is nothing new about the thousands of tigers and other exotic animals in captivity. History provides a long and disturbing narrative about the global reach of the exotic animal trade over thousands of years. While "menagerie" is a term that hails from the seventeenth century and "zoo" from the nineteenth, humans have always held exotic animals in captivity. Royal families and powerful leaders have long used wild beasts, heavily freighted with symbolic meaning, to reinforce mastery and supremacy over their domains. Circumnavigation of the globe and the subsequent seventeenth century expansion of shipping routes and international commerce created a boom in the exotic animal trade as wild animals were captured and shipped around the world. Over the course of the nineteenth century, naturalists and scientists began to create the forerunners of the modern zoo. Acreage in Regent's Park was set aside for what would become the London Zoo and other zoos followed in Dublin, Berlin, Melbourne, New York City's Central Park, and around the globe. Urbanites could not get enough of them then, and the same appears to hold today.

Modern zoos are among the most popular of family entertainments and their popularity shows no signs of diminishing. Approximately 200 million people visit an accredited zoo each year in America, according to the Association of Zoos and Aquariums (AZA). AZA accredits 240 zoos and aquariums around the world, including 217 in the United States and 23 in twelve other countries. Accredited zoos enable people to see the wild animals that bring wonder to our world without having to travel to Africa, Asia, Australia, or other distant lands and are important participants in species preservation and conservation.

Zoos are partially driven by an interest in showing visitors as many species as possible. Astonishingly, AZA-accredited zoos house a total of 800,000 animals, including 6,000 species and 1,000 threatened or endangered species. Problematically, they are often found in urban areas without room to expand their acreage. As examples, the Houston Zoo houses 6,000 animals on 55 acres; the Bronx Zoo 6,000 animals on 265 acres; and the Toronto Zoo 5,000 on 700 acres. Based on these statistics, the animals per acre for these zoos are Houston – 109; Bronx – 23; Toronto – 7. Consider also that some (often significant) portion of a zoo's property is given over to amphitheaters and exhibit areas, rides and play areas, retail outlets and restaurants – which suggests the animal acreage is smaller and the animals per acre ratio even higher than estimated above. While the animal to acreage ratio undoubtedly oversimplifies the complexity of zoo operations, particularly given the type and complement of animals housed at a particular facility (clearly a tarantula needs less room than a tiger), it nonetheless underscores the reality that many, if not most, zoos are landlocked and overcrowded, and animals may suffer for it.

In truth, zoos are built as much – or more – for their visitors as for the animals they keep. While AZA-accredited zoos are strongly committed to creating naturalistic and interesting spaces for their wild denizens and improving animal welfare through enrichment methods, they must balance the physical and psychological well-being of their captive animal residents with that of their public entertainment and education mission. As Vicki Croke has written in *The Modern Ark*, "While the zoo can be an intriguing place to visit, it can be an awfully boring place to live." Even well-cared for captive animals can experience loneliness, monotony, and stress.

Enclosures are often designed to be shallow, so the tiger, lion, or cheetah cannot hide from visitors. Energetic wild cats biologically programmed to race after prey barely have enough room to get up a good trot. Bears genetically encoded to forage for food across hundreds of miles are confined to cages the size of a living room. Den doors are often closed during the day, so animals have no retreat from the public view. Great crowds of people at eye level are constant stressors. Captive wild animals are unable to defend their territories against the pressure of the intrusive crowd. They can neither fight nor flee.

When their psychological distress becomes unbearable, caged animals begin to exhibit what are called stereotypic behaviors, a condition sometimes called "zoochosis" because of its pervasiveness in zoos. Stereotypic behaviors are repetitive, unchanging, abnormal behavior patterns with no obvious goal or function, which are often associated with extremely poor emotional and psychological well-being. Have you ever watched a tiger or a lion endlessly pace back and forth from one end of its tiny cage to the other? Or seen a bear walk slowly and methodically along one wall of its enclosure and, when it arrives at the corner, suddenly raise up on its hind legs, twist its neck, and twirl its body around to retrace its steps? Nor is it only large carnivores who suffer. Elephants rock and sway in place. Giraffes bite or suck on the high bars of their compounds. Primates curl into fetal positions, eyes downcast, and arms clenched around their torsos in a defensive embrace against the dark world surrounding them. Some captive wild animals over-groom or self-mutilate, biting or chewing on legs or tails. Almost all pace and pace and pace in a trance-like daze, oblivious to other stimuli and completely disconnected from the outside world. These are all stereotypic coping mechanisms – and they do nothing to alleviate the animal's pain.

Bears are particularly vulnerable to stereotypical behaviors because of their need to constantly be on the move. They also are among the hardest species to break of repetitive fixations. Even when the stressors are removed, the bear often continues its abnormal behavior patterns, as we observed with Kody, a large brown bear rescued by the Sanctuary.

Kody was initially housed in a large and luxurious habitat chock full of trees for shade, rocks for climbing, and a sizable pond for swimming and soaking. He took advantage of these features, bobbing around in the pool and sunbathing on the boulders. But he would occasionally walk over to the southwest corner of his habitat and begin a measured, deliberate, and compulsive routine. He would pace twelve steps west along the fence to the corner. Then he would turn right and take twelve steps along the fence to the north. He would reverse direction and pace twelve steps back to the corner. He would turn left and take twelve steps back along the fence to his starting point. Then he would turn and start the process again. Pace. Turn. About face. Pace. Turn. About face. Repeat. Repeat. Repeat.

Kody followed this route so often that his enormous feet and great bulk created deep impressions in the soft soil, and he would carefully step into his own footprints, up one side, turn, down the other side, turn, repeat. Kent Drotar determined that the length of Kody's path on each side mimicked the size of the cage in which he lived prior to being rescued by the Sanctuary. Even though Kody had room to roam and a playground full of toys he continued to engage in mindless pacing from time to time – until, as we will soon see, he began to make some new friends.

Used, Abused, and Abandoned: Making Money Off of Exotic Animals

If even some of America's most illustrious zoological parks have too many animals and too little space, what must life be like for exotic animals living in small, nonaccredited roadside zoos, bear pits, circuses, and other similar setups? Not all commercial, for-profit wild animal businesses are low-quality, poorly-run operations. But it is impossible to ignore the cruelty inflicted by many captive animal outfits. With apologies to any well-run facility that places animal well-being above all else, in truth, "roadside zoos" and "bear pits" have become pejorative terms because the owners of such facilities have earned it.

Roadside Zoos

Cricket Hollow Animal Park. Tri-State Zoological Park. Deer Haven Mini Zoo. These are names that bring a shudder to even the most seasoned Sanctuary rescue teams, who have experienced the most deplorable of what are loosely termed "roadside zoos," small commercial and too-often decrepit businesses that make money off exotic animals. It is difficult to determine how many such operations exist across the U.S. Estimates range from as few as 500 to as many as 3,000.

Originally positioned alongside highways to attract passing motorists in the 1960s, today they may also be located alongside strip malls or next to retail shops and restaurants where tourists or locals congregate. Roadside zoos often operate on shoestring budgets, confining wild animals to tiny, barren cages without enough food, clean water, or veterinary care over their entire, often short, and forever miserable, lives. Pat Craig describes them this way:

> Usually, these so-called zoos start with a small assortment of animals that someone collected in their backyard and when they finally have enough interested friends and relatives coming by to see them, they typically decide to throw open the doors and start charging admission for people to visit. We've seen many variations of this concept over the years and they all seem to share a common theme such as small cages, cramped quarters, low-budget building materials, inadequate cleaning routines, poor nutrition, make-shift accommodations, and so on. They almost always have owners that are comfortable with their creations, no matter how substandard the conditions are for the animals.

The Sanctuary rescued Jumanji, a black leopard, from a roadside zoo in Ohio, where he was confined to an outdoor cage in the frigid Midwest winter. This big cat of the tropics suffered ammonia burns from lying in his own urine and agonizing frostbite from brutally cold conditions. He came to the Sanctuary with unchecked infections from his open wounds. Since recovering, Jumanji has become a stunningly beautiful big cat who can be seen strolling majestically through the large leopard habitat.

3.1 Jumanji shortly after arriving at the Sanctuary

3.2 Jumanji fully recovered in the leopard habitat

Among the most notorious roadside zoo operators was Joe Exotic, as documented in *Tiger King*. He was charged with shooting five tigers in the head because they could no longer be bred. Then he threw their carcasses in the garbage. He was investigated for the mysterious deaths of almost two dozen tiger cubs over a seven-month period and falsified government documents to throw federal agents off his trail. Then, in April 2019 Joe Exotic was found guilty of seventeen wildlife charges and a murder-for-hire plot targeting a captive big cat activist and was sentenced to twenty-two years behind bars.

Pits, Prisons, and Publicity Stunts

The bear pits of North Carolina, Tennessee, Georgia, and other locations in the southeastern United States provide another opportunity for tourists to ogle brown bears in barren concrete holes. Perhaps inspired by Bern, Switzerland's original tourist attraction, which has housed successive generations of the city's brown bear mascots since 1857, these operations are dank and cramped pits with sheer concrete walls and floors. In 2013 the Sanctuary rescued seventeen black and grizzly bears from the Black Forest Bear Park in Helen, Georgia and has since collaborated with the Captive Animal Law Enforcement arm of People for the Ethical Treatment of Animals (PETA) in the rescues of more than seventy bears from other, similar circumstances.

3.3 Bear pit bear begging for food

Some bears are imprisoned, not in pits, but behind bars. Fifi was a Syrian brown bear, a slightly smaller cousin of the American brown bear. She was one of four bears used to perform tricks in a derelict, family-owned roadside zoo and languished behind bars for three decades. At the Sanctuary, Fifi, the thirty-year old arthritic bruin with the haunted

3.4 Fifi before she was rescued   3.5 Fifi after her first hibernation

countenance, became a great furry wonder with a thick luxurious coat, robust gait, and great bulk.

Yoya, a tiger, was confined to a tiny cage in her owner's blue jean factory in Mexico for twenty long years. When the Sanctuary team first saw her, Pat recalls, "Instead of seeing eyes that possessed a glimmer of hope, Yoya responded with a look that said she was ready to die." Too weak to fly to Colorado, Yoya was given round the clock care, including being hand fed a rich and healthy diet at a partner animal care facility in Pachuca, Mexico. Yoya finally made the trip to Colorado in early 2016 to live out her life in comfort and tranquility.

3.6 Yoya before she was rescued   3.7 Yoya at the Sanctuary

As bad or worse may be the all-too-common scenarios where the exotic animal is used as a "publicity stunt" or a "gimmick." African lion Leonardo, who was Pat's first international rescue, spent his life in a rusty cage on the sidewalk outside a fortune teller's shop in Puebla, Mexico to lure pedestrians inside. Negrita, a jet black female jaguar, also came to the

Sanctuary from Mexico. Her owner, known as "Pepe Tigre," set up cages around the tables of his Cancun restaurant so cruise ship passengers could sit next to a caged lion, tiger, or jaguar while enjoying their meals. When Hurricane Wilma hit, the owner fled the scene and most of the animals drowned. He took Negrita with him so he could use her as a prop to beg for money; he later let her loose in the jungle where she almost starved to death.

The Sanctuary rescued Ricki, a black bear, from an ice cream shop in Pennsylvania that encouraged patrons to feed dog food to the caged bruin before swinging into the ice cream shop for some Rocky Road. "Hi, I'm Little Ricki," read the cheery little sign outside the cage, "I'm a 215 lb. female PA black bear. I was born in Feb. 1996." When Sanctuary rescuers first saw that sign, Ricki had been caged outside the ice cream shop for nineteen years. Patrons paid a trivial amount to feed Ricki dog kibble through a plastic chute. Public outrage, a lawsuit by the Animal Legal Defense Fund, and an online petition signed by almost 200,000 people resulted in her release. Ricki now enjoys the company of half a dozen older female black bears at the Sanctuary. She has become a world class hibernator, perhaps making up for nineteen years without a good winter's sleep.

3.8 Ricki at the ice cream shop   3.9 Ricki at the Sanctuary

Circuses

Fed by a growing public backlash, circuses started closing (or shutting down their animal acts) about a decade ago. The public outrage was well justified; circus animals often experience the worst of abusive situations. Morelia, an African lion, was rescued by the Sanctuary from a circus in Mexico, where a scantily clad Tarzan-wannabe would swing into the ring and club her over the head until she was unconscious. Morelia eventually became too weak to play her part, so she was bred repeatedly only to have her cubs taken from her shortly after they were born. When authorities came to confiscate the circus's animals she was hidden in a trailer without food and water. By chance she was discovered a few days later, close to death. Morelia, who was in her twenties when she was rescued by the Sanctuary, moved into a spacious "Assisted Living" area in the Lion House, content to eat magnificently, sleep profusely, and enjoy the activity around her.

3.10 Morelia before she was rescued   3.11 Morelia at the Sanctuary

In 2009, Bolivia was the first South American country to pass a law banning the use of wild and domestic animals in circuses; twenty-five circus lions rescued from Bolivia were given new homes at the Sanctuary. Almost every other Central and South American country and most European countries have issued nationwide bans on the use of animals or wild animals in circuses, and the momentum continues to build. In a major victory for animal rights defenders, Ringling Bros. and Barnum & Bailey Circus, arguably the world's most well-known circus and long advertised as "The Greatest Show on Earth," closed its doors in May of 2017. Although the United States has not passed a nationwide ban on circuses there are nearly one hundred partial or full bans in thirty-two states.

Pay-to-Play and the Breeding Rings that Perpetuate the Problem

Among the worst exotic animal "entertainments" are those that encourage human-animal contact, which almost always takes place with small cubs. These "pay-to-play" petting and photo schemes need a constant supply of small cubs (tiger, lion, jaguar, leopard, bear, whatever) because the cubs bring in the tourists and the money. Tourists pay $20, $50, even $100 or more to pet, pass around, or have their pictures taken with cute furry helpless cubs. Doc Antle's Myrtle Beach Safari, a much more sophisticated operation, charges $339 per person for a three-hour guided walking tour during which tourists can feed an African elephant, "interact with baby tiger cubs," meet a cheetah, "and so much more!" Plus, in the age of the

3.12 Pay-to-play cub petting
At least four tiger cubs can be seen here with a room full of tourists.

ubiquitous selfie, the owner of the cubs does not even have to go to the trouble or expense of procuring and setting up photography equipment. All he or she must do is provide the prop – a young cub that was torn away from its mother a few weeks or even a few days after it was born. Unthinking tourists seem more than happy to take a selfie and impress their friends with a picture on Facebook or Instagram. Sadly, few people consider the fact that the cub is miserable and deprived of solitude and sleep, not to mention the loss of maternal care.

While playing with cubs is dreadful, swimming with tiger cubs at Dade City's Wild Things, a now-shuttered roadside zoo in Florida, was even worse. There, frightened cubs who had not yet learned how to swim, or were too exhausted to do so, were forced into swimming pools with splashing tourists. Ultimately, Dade City's was cited for more than forty Animal Welfare Act violations and was sued by PETA for violations of the Endangered Species Act. Upon concluding a two-year undercover investigation into captive tigers with photographer Steve Winter, journalist Sharon Guynup noted that "Dade City's Wild Things...had some of the smallest cages and most concerning conditions I saw in any of the 30-some roadside zoos we visited." After their license was suspended by the USDA, the owner made arrangements with Joe Exotic to move nineteen tigers to Oklahoma before a scheduled PETA inspection. As Brittany Peet, Deputy General Counsel, Captive Animal Law Enforcement at the PETA Foundation recalls, the tigers were "moved in the middle of July on an extremely hot day in a metal cattle trailer with no climate control...and no water receptacles. One of the tigers gave birth to three cubs on the trip and all three died." The Wild Animal Sanctuary team rescued the nineteen tigers (along with twenty more) from Joe Exotic's zoo in 2017, and then drove to Florida for the last six tigers at Dade City's when the business finally closed in the spring of 2020.

Captive wildlife breeding operations deliberately proliferate the problem because that is where the money is. Why do the "petters" never

3.13 Swimming with a tiger cub at Dade City's Wild Things

3.14 Swimming with a tiger cub at Dade City's Wild Things

ask where the cubs that they are passing around like party favors come from? Or what happens to the animals when they become too large and dangerous to fondle? In answer to the first question, we suspect you have heard of puppy mills. But have you heard of tiger mills? Tigers are most often abused in cub petting ploys because they breed well in captivity. In the wild, a female tiger will give birth to cubs only every two to three years. In captivity a female tiger will be bred two or even three times over the course of a year for the better part of a decade or more. But tigers are not alone; breeding operations can be found for most of the big cat species, and to a lesser extent, bears. The point is if an exotic animal can be bred, it will be bred.

It is a vicious circle. Tiger mills (and other large carnivore breeding operations) feed the demand for the "props" needed in pay-to-play outfits who must in turn satisfy tourists flocking in to pet and photograph the "props." Given the exceedingly short "shelf life" of a tiger or lion or bear cub, the exploiters must keep replacing the "disposable" babies with newer "models." Or, in the words of Steve Winter, they are swapped out upon reaching their "expiration date," at about twelve to sixteen weeks of age. The cubs may then be sold to other roadside zoos, circuses, and entertainment venues, or they may be killed. The self-perpetuating and lucrative cub breeding scheme is what Sharon Guynup calls the "breed – pet – dump – cubs business model...The driver of the cub petting industry." The bottom line is that cubs feed the bottom line: a single baby tiger can bring in thousands of dollars over the course of a summer tourist season.

Tourists are often told that the money they fork out to pet a lion cub or take a tiger selfie – or even visit adult wild animals in a roadside zoo or a bear pit – is going to conserve animal species in danger of extinction. The truth is people unwittingly contribute to captive wildlife cruelty, not conservation, when they support wildlife exploiters who profess to be wildlife protectors. There is no legitimate conservation reason for breeding or owning captive wild animals. Those who claim otherwise are motivated not by wildlife conservation but by arrogance, money, misconception, or all the above. In the first place, even if someone were willing to spend the money to raise the cubs to adulthood and then transport them halfway around the world to repopulate their native lands, the animals could not be released into the wild. Hunting is instinctive but hunting success in a specific biome is a learned behavior passed down from mother to cubs. In addition, many captive animals who live to adulthood have been declawed, defanged, or had their teeth filed down to nubs to protect the humans who hold them captive. The chances of survival for a large carnivore without claws and/or teeth are almost none. And, since they have been fed by humans their entire lives, captive animals have "imprinted" on people and have no fear of them, making them more dangerous in human-animal interactions. Finally, many if not most captive large carnivores outside of zoos are genetically-inferior hybrids, which, if released into the wild, could weaken a wild population that may have evolved over thousands of years or more.

Tigers are the classic example of species hybridization. You have probably heard of Bengal tigers and Siberian tigers and maybe Sumatran tigers. But we doubt you have heard of "generic" tigers. Generic tigers are the mutts of the big cat world and they make up about ninety-five percent of captive tigers in the U.S. In legitimate conservation programs at AZA-accredited zoos, animal keepers are careful, through record keeping and DNA tests, to breed within subspecies, such as Bengals to Bengals and Siberians to Siberians. Unprincipled breeders of captive tigers, however, have no such scruples. Commercial breeders of tigers could not care less about genetic safeguarding. They have been selling, swapping, and profiting from anything with an orange and black striped coat, or even better a white coat, for decades.

White tigers are often glamorized and romanticized but they often suffer from severe birth defects and serious health problems that result in part from the whiteness gene and in part from the inbreeding necessary to harness that gene. The gene that causes white pigmentation in tigers is associated with optical birth defects and white tigers are routinely born with crossed-eyes and other vision problems. But the bigger white tiger problem is inbreeding. There are so few tigers with the whiteness gene, ruthless breeders know that the only way to produce white tigers is through excessive inbreeding: mothers to sons, fathers to daughters, brothers to sisters, and so on. As a result, white tigers are rarely born without birth defects such as spinal and facial deformities. They also suffer from kidney disease, pulmonary problems, and compromised immune systems. White tigers are not glamorous; they are excessively inbred genetic aberrations.

Diego, an enormous white and black striped tiger, was rescued by the Sanctuary from a Mexican resort that purchased him as a cub for use in tourist photo ops. If Diego had been an orange tiger, the resort could easily have replaced him with another orange cub. But white tigers are hard to come by and they are expensive. So, the resort hung onto Diego for years, removing his claws to reduce the danger to the tourists and keeping him constantly sedated so resort guests could take their pictures with him. Today, Diego lives in a habitat all his own next to tiger neighbors at the Sanctuary.

Hybrids have become the new designer "doodles," if you will, of the big cat world. It is not just a matter of breeding generic tigers or inbreeding to engineer white tigers. Breeders are turning with increasing frequency to interbreeding species. A male lion and a female tiger will bag you a liger. A male tiger and a female lion will get you a tigon. Why stop there? A male lion and a female liger will produce liligers. Of course, leopard, jaguars, cougars, and all sorts of similar big cats are also being brought into the mix; it is simply a matter of working out the moniker for the offspring. Accredited zoos prohibit the breeding of generic tigers, white tigers, and mixed species, but that does not stop exploiters out to make a buck. There is no legitimate reason to hybridize big cats – but there is no law to effectively stop the practice either. In fact, current laws do not even come close to solving the problems of exotic animal trafficking and trade.

There Oughta be a Law

How are exotic pets, roadside zoos, bear pits, circuses, petting schemes, and tiger mills even possible, you ask? Are there no laws in place that deal with these problems? Surprisingly, there is little federal oversight or consistent enforcement brought to bear on the captive wildlife crisis overall. As exemplified by the trespasser-meets-tiger-in-a-Houston-house story, law enforcement and legal advancements tend to be knee-jerk reactions. Stumble upon a tiger, send in a SWAT team. Again, the Houston tiger was lucky. Not so for forty-eight large carnivores owned by Terry Thompson of Zanesville, Ohio, a debacle that gets to the crux of the problem.

Terry Thompson's release of more than fifty exotic animals into the Zanesville, Ohio countryside before committing suicide has become the unhinged-exotic-animal-owner-tale heard round the world. On October 18, 2011, Thompson opened the cage doors of his exotics and then he killed himself. With homes, an apartment building, and a school in the area, the order from the Sheriff's department was to shoot any animal who was loose. When the carnage came to a stop, eighteen tigers, seventeen African lions, six black bears, two grizzly bears, three cougars and two wolves were dead. Ohio legislators ultimately passed some of the toughest exotic animal ownership laws in the country. Since then, The Wild Animal Sanctuary has rescued numerous large carnivores in Ohio from owners now forced to surrender their wild animals. Among these are four African lions, Leo, Leon, Zoya, and Zinna who once belonged to Terry Thompson.

Although Ohio, whose legislators were stunned into action by the possible loss of human life in Zanesville, and some other states have passed tough wild animal ownership laws, state and local laws are a complete muddle – and one that seems to be in an ongoing state of flux. There are about twenty states that completely ban the ownership of dangerous exotic animals, including wild cats and bears, whether for personal edification or commercial enterprise. At the other end of the spectrum are the four states –Alabama, Nevada, North Carolina, and Wisconsin – which have no laws prohibiting keeping dangerous wild animals as pets. The remaining states are somewhere in between.

To make matters worse, there is *no* federal law in the United States that bans the ownership of big cats, bears, and other exotic animals. The laws that do exist lack regulatory muscle. They are rife with grandfather clauses and other exemptions that prolong egregious practices. Regulations are also inconsistent, allowed to lapse without renewals, and erratically enforced. In short, federal laws fail to adequately protect the health and safety of the public or the well-being of captive wild animals. Moreover, none solve the captive wildlife problem because, quite simply, none ban ownership or breeding – and that is the real problem.

The underlying premise of the U.S. federal laws dealing with captive wildlife is that exotic animal ownership is acceptable. The government merely needs to manage the movement and safety of tigers, say, across state lines as they would any commercial product, like broccoli or bunk beds. So, federal laws address the import/export, transport, and buying, selling, or otherwise acquiring wildlife and set minimum animal welfare standards for those engaged in such activities.

To that end, the USDA issues licenses for commercial enterprises who buy, sell, trade, and breed wild animals. Although the USDA does not require private owners of exotic animals to obtain licenses, some owners do because it enables them to take advantage of a regulatory loophole. You see, some states ban wild animal pets, but if the owner holds a USDA exhibitor license, he or she is exempt from state laws. Currently, a USDA license will put you out $10 for the application fee and from $30 to $300 in annual fees, depending on the number of animals you own (the $300 maximum is levied for those who own more than 500 animals). An animal license for one exotic animal costs little more than a dog license in most states and five hundred wild animals can be yours for less than the cost of license plates for your car. Federal law exemptions enable people to circumvent state laws and may push people into exhibiting to cover the enormous costs of captive animal ownership. The process is simple. Locate the loophole, do the math, apply for the license.

Regardless of the laws on – or not on – the books, the fact is, wild animals suffer in captivity – they are bred in captivity, born in captivity, and will die in captivity. Majestic animals may be starved, drugged, addicted to nicotine for training purposes, beaten, and left to die. Many have never lived outside of small, barren cages in which they can barely turn around. They may never have seen another of their species. Some have lived knee deep in urine and excrement. Joint, muscle, and foot problems are rampant from lives spent on concrete floors. Roughly sixty percent of Sanctuary rescues have been declawed and/or defanged; some have had most, or all their teeth pulled or filed down to nubs on the premise that they would be less likely to injure their owners. Many have been imprisoned in garages, basements, crawl spaces, barns, or trailers their entire lives.

While the physical abuses are horrific, the emotional and psychological cruelties may be even worse. Jan Creamer, co-founder, CEO, and President of Animal Defenders International (ADI) understands deeply the emotional suffering of these animals. In the film *Lion Ark*, which documents ADI's rescue of twenty-five lions from Bolivia who were airlifted to The Wild Animal Sanctuary in 2011, she spoke about a lion named Colo Colo:

> When we do investigations it's the violence that people notice but the deprivation these animals endure would break any of us... just think about what you have done in the last twelve years of your life – the places you've visited, changed jobs, homes, made new friends, fallen in love, parents may have seen their children become teenagers. Colo Colo spent all of those years in this cage...

Colo Colo lived for twelve years in a nine by twelve foot cage in Bolivia. Yoya for twenty in Mexico. Ricki for nineteen in Pennsylvania. Yet, amidst the sadness of the captive wildlife crisis and the suffering of animals who have been through more than most of us could bear, there are the uplifting stories of the lucky ones rescued by The Wild Animal Sanctuary.

You will be pleased to know that Kody's pacing has abated, and he enjoys swimming in his pool and visiting his new neighbors, senior-citizen grizzly bears Walter and Mafalda. As for Colo Colo, the angry lion from Bolivia? Once at the Sanctuary, animal caregivers discovered that Colo Colo's anger at being imprisoned was amplified by excruciating pain – from a major toothache. A dental team led by Dr. Peter Emily of the Peter Emily International Veterinary Dental Foundation quickly rectified the problem with root canal therapy.

3.15 Kody relaxing in the pool

These lions and bears and leopards and tigers are among more than 1,000 animals rescued by the Sanctuary over the course of forty years. After suffering for most of their lives, they continuously astound with their ability to accept kindness, demonstrate resilience, muster a vast reservoir of inner strength, and reveal an indomitable *will to live*. Each has a story to tell about how he or she found "sanctuary" at the Sanctuary, a haven for rescued animals who are provided high quality and humane care, and a safe home for the rest of their natural lives. It is a place, above all, where the animals come first and where they are treated with respect, dignity, and love. It is what was stirring in the back of Pat Craig's mind when he started Boulder Zoological Inc. forty years ago.

But we get ahead of ourselves. In order to truly appreciate the mission, success, and significance of The Wild Animal Sanctuary in shaping large carnivore rescue and rehabilitation, we must first go back to the Valmont family farm, and then move to Lyons, relocate to Keenesburg, and come forward to the present day.

Chapter 4

● ● ● ● ● ● ● ● ● ● ● ● ● ● ● ●

Prairie Homecoming: A Sanctuary on the Move

In 1986 Pat Craig was running out of space for wild animals at the family farm on Valmont Road. With about twenty large carnivores now in his care, he needed to explore other options. This would be the first time Pat would have to move his growing animal sanctuary, but it would not be the last.

He found a new property just east of Lyons nestled on the edge of the Front Range foothills. Lyons is a tiny town lying at the confluence of North and South Saint Vrain Creeks about fifteen miles north of Boulder. A quaint reminder of Colorado's homesteading and farming history, Lyons serves as a distant gateway to Rocky Mountain National Park, located about twenty miles to the northwest. The town is famous for its sandstone, a red and salmon colored rock that is among the hardest in the world and a popular building, paving, and patio product.

Pat's newfound property was adjacent to a large area of Boulder County Open Space land on one side and farmland on the other side. Although a substantial part of the neighbor's farmland was irrigated, there remained a large unirrigated parcel. As is typical in Colorado, where there is no water, there are a "million prairie dogs." With all the prairie dog holes, it was impossible to graze cattle, so the farmer allowed Pat to fence in the immense parcel for his large carnivores. Pat knew the big cats and bears would not be bothered by the hundreds of holes that pock-marked the pasture or by sharing their space with scores of diminutive rodents. It was a fabulous set up. Mostly pasture, with woods along the western edge, the animals could play in the sun or seek the shade of large trees.

Applying what he had learned over the past six years, Pat settled in to manage his wildlife operation, as well as two service stations in nearby Longmont that funded the whole enterprise. He was putting in long days that typically began at 4:00 a.m. and ended around 6:00 p.m. at the service station. At that point he would head for home and spend another six or eight hours caring for the animals. Part of the nightly routine involved playtime in the enormous fenced field. Some people come home from work and walk their dogs. Pat walked his African lions.

I didn't just leave them out there...I was always out there when there were animals in that 1,000 acres. All I did, every day, was take turns, walk for a couple of hours with a pride of lions, let them play around, sit out there with them. There was a big irrigation ditch out there and they played in the water and under the trees. Then they would get tired, and I'd be saying, "No, no, you can't go to sleep here." So we would walk back. They didn't want to stay out by themselves...When we went back, they were really happy to go in their cages and take a big nap. Then I'd take somebody else out. Back then I did a lot of walking.

The days were long, and the work was hard, but the whole set up was functional and immensely fulfilling. As he says, "We were there for eight years and during that time I was really starting to get a hang of the whole captive wildlife problem and how we fit into it." Pat kept rescuing animals, expanding the compound, and making a name for himself and what was now called Rocky Mountain Wildlife Conservation Center. By the early 1990s, he had about forty animals under his care.

But before Pat knew it, it was time to move yet again. In 1993 a concrete company began strip mining for shale, establishing a quarry operation right up to the fence line of his property. The blasting was so loud it shook the house. It also shook up the animals. The hunt for new land was on.

Prairie Homecoming

If you were looking for a place large enough for an animal sanctuary that was home to a few dozen large wild carnivores – African lions, tigers, leopards, jaguars, mountain lions, black bears, and more – where would you put it? It is not an easy question. And it was not easy to find an answer when in 1994 Pat Craig needed to move his animals from the foothills near Lyons. He wanted to stay in Colorado, but where?

When people think of Colorado, they think mountains. With fifty separate mountain ranges, Colorado boasts six times the mountainous area of Switzerland, fifty-four majestic peaks over 14,000 feet, and three of the four tallest peaks in the lower forty-eight. The Rocky Mountains – wild, magnificent, and mythical – have been the stuff of legends since early explorers, fur trappers and gold seekers, and later homesteaders and settlers made their way across the western United States. With splendid national parks and national forests, the Rockies remain a major source of American cultural identity and a tourist mecca today.

All true, but what is habitually overlooked is that roughly forty percent of Colorado is short-grass prairie. Gently rolling plains cover the eastern part of the state, rising slowly and imperceptibly from the neighboring states of Kansas and Nebraska. Twenty-seven million acres of short grass prairie represent the final groundswell of the Great Plains grasslands that begins west of the Mississippi River and blankets the central United States before breaking upon the bulwark of the Rocky Mountains.

In the early nineteenth century the expanse of land from west of the Mississippi to the Rocky Mountains so shocked European immigrants accustomed to wooded glens and dense forests, it was labeled the "Great American Desert." The characterization was not that far off. Areas in the United States that receive eight inches or less of precipitation are classified as desert. Lying in the rain shadow of the mountains, Colorado's dry, high altitude, semi-arid eastern plains receive only twelve inches of rainfall or less annually.

The Colorado prairie is an austere and humble landscape, as unassuming in appearance as the mountains to its west are magnificent. Decidedly flat, with only a few bumps and dips to break the monotony, and mostly bereft of trees whose moisture requirements substantially exceed the rainfall limits, this is a harsh yet fragile environment which suffers brutally cold winters, life threatening blizzards, and frequent droughts. Snows drift high in winter. Flash floods are not uncommon in spring. Arroyos dry up in summer. Fires periodically scorch the land. The sun bakes this landlocked semi-desert more than three hundred days a year. The winds blow consistently; sometimes it seems they blow constantly.

There are few landmarks of note. A mesa as flat as a kitchen table. A rugged butte. A sharp edged arroyo. Prairie grasses that ripple and sway in sharp winds. Fields of golden wheat, glossy green corn stalks, ruffled furrows of sorghum fields carve this planar panorama into an abstract canvas of immense sun-washed circles and squares. Distance is deceptive. Time is elusive. Herds of cattle, ponderously munching the meager offerings from patch to patch of prairie grass never seem to go anywhere, perhaps realizing that the grass is most definitely *not* greener on the other side. The few trees, mostly cottonwoods, follow paltry watercourses, or man-made irrigation ditches. Relief from the fierce sun is delivered only by passing clouds, which can gather with alarming speed in the afternoon and unleash torrential downpours.

Let's face it. Aesthetically speaking, short grass prairie, in a word, comes up short. We thrill to the Rocky Mountains' soaring peaks, rocky outcroppings, endless variety, bold vistas, and monumental scale. We seek breathtaking views and awe inspiring panoramas. Even our pastoral preferences lean toward the verdant and wooded hills and hollows of the eastern United States, preferably populated by quietly grazing herds of contented sheep and cattle. These are the landscapes we have been taught to love – not what most people see as a lackluster, sage-colored, featureless flatland.

Yet the short grass prairie is a miracle of ecological adaptation that teems with life (albeit not as much as it used to) and a glorious and subtle beauty all its own. Grasslands, it seems, are best appreciated on foot or better yet on horseback, swaying in the saddle at an easy walk. For this is a beauty that demands close observation, infinite patience, and attention to detail. Everything is low to the ground. A twisted blade of grass, a tiny prairie phlox flower, mogul-towns of prairie dog mounds. Colorado's largest ecosystem, the eastern plains are home to more than 200 plant and animal species. Drought-resistant Buffalo Grass and blue grama hang on to every drop of moisture, driving root systems deep into the soil. Mule deer and pronghorn antelope graze the bluffs and follow the muddy, ephemeral streams that come and go with the whims of weather. Eagles, hawks, owls, and a variety of songbirds are just a few of the birds that populate the area. Less spectacular lizards, snakes, jackrabbits, western rattlers, and prairie dogs burrow beneath the surface.

The biggest animals are long gone. Before they were hunted to near extinction, at least twenty million hump-backed bison (some put the estimate closer to seventy million) blackened the plains. Gigantic herds of elk, mule deer, and pronghorn antelopes grazed the land. Gray wolves, which may have numbered in the hundreds of thousands, followed the food supply, as did mountain lions, which also roamed the plains. Grizzlies, too, once ranged throughout the land but have not been seen here in over a century. As always, the demise of prey occasioned the departure of predators and the wolves, mountain lions, and grizzlies disappeared long ago.

Most see Colorado's eastern plains as miles of empty monotony – or simply do not see them at all. This is fly-over country to those making their way from coast to coast or to Colorado's fabled ski resorts. Seen from 35,000 feet it is little more than geometry, a patchwork of pivot-irrigation circles and strip-farming rectangles. Tourists driving in from the east at eighty miles an hour on Interstate 70 can barely contain their rising exasperation with the 200-miles of prairie tedium they must endure to reach the splendor of the mountains beyond. Even those whose families have lived here for generations are moving away to better opportunities in bigger cities. The eastern plains have been losing population for decades.

Indeed, for most of us, short-grass prairie is a place to drive *through*, not *to*, a place to move away *from*, not a place to move *to*.

That is, of course, unless you are a captive wildlife champion with more than enough large carnivores to fill a small zoo. For Pat Craig, the prairie worked just fine. The fewer the people, the better. Lightly settled and surrounded by dirt tracks and big farms and ranches in the early 1990s, the eastern plains had yet to be swallowed up by the suburban sprawl transforming Denver, Boulder, and other Front Range cities and towns. Although a few more hills and trees admittedly would have improved the picturesque quality of the land, fencing would be considerably easier to build on loamy flatland soil than in the mountains where gulches, granite, and rock outcroppings confound every attempt. Nights are hushed and the blue-black sky is glazed with stars, all the better to enjoy the roar of African lions, who would feel right at home in a land reminiscent of the African savannah. The black bears would adapt, as would the tigers, providing they had water to play around in. As for the mountain lions – and the grizzly bears and gray wolves that Pat would later add to his complement of large carnivores – well, they would be coming home to the prairie for the first time in more than a century.

4.1 Sanctuary grizzlies...

4.2 wolves, and...

4.3 a magnificent mountain lion

So, in 1994, the founder of The Wild Animal Sanctuary brought about forty large carnivores to 160 acres of prairie near Keenesburg, Colorado. Since then more than 1.5 million visitors have followed him here. We were among those visitors whose eyes were opened to the work of a *true* animal sanctuary.

Chapter 5

🐾 🐾 🐾 🐾 🐾 🐾 🐾 🐾 🐾 🐾 🐾 🐾 🐾 🐾 🐾 🐾
🐾 🐾 🐾 🐾 🐾 🐾 🐾 🐾 🐾 🐾 🐾 🐾 🐾 🐾 🐾 🐾

A True Sanctuary:
Where Animals Set the Agenda

We have been strolling the Mile into the Wild Walkway at the Sanctuary for a couple of hours. It is mid-July and the breeze is hot, the air is dry, and the sun is intense. We have spotted at least twenty-five African lions amid the long summer grasses – and not one of them has moved. Well, okay, one lioness lazily raised her head. If you need a poster child for utter repose, look no further. The lions are stretched out as far as possible from nose to tail, every inch of their lithe bodies pressed into the tall grass in a vain attempt to catch any bit of coolness that might be radiating from the ground. Others are congregated in a heap under shade canopies. Some are engaged in what we have come to call "synchronized sleeping." African lions are so imitative of each other's behaviors that it is not unusual to see four or five of them sleeping together in the exact same position: lying on their right sides, heads pointed in the same direction, tails stretched out like long exclamation points behind. If one lifts its head, the others do too. Wherever we look, there are lions sprawled on their backs, bellies baking in the sun, hind legs dangling lazily. All are out for the count.

So, today we have seen lions, but we really have not *seen* lions. This is life at the Sanctuary. Sometimes you see animals. Sometimes you do not. The big cats may be roaming, playing, eating, chasing through the meadows, or engaged in a gloriously orchestrated chorus of roars – but often they are simply sleeping, not unlike their wild cousins in Africa. Here, above all else, the animals set their own agendas.

And that is the key difference between a zoo and a true animal sanctuary. Zoos are built mostly for the people who visit them. Sanctuaries are built for the animals who live in them. Pat Craig, the staff, and volunteers must on occasion gently remind visitors of this reality. Frequent

5.1 Hercules' pride

visitors may be disappointed if a favorite is asleep in its den. First timers might be frustrated because the animals are not particularly active. Still others wish the animals were closer so they could see them better. But the Sanctuary is not about us, it is all about the rescued animals who live here. "The Wild Animal Sanctuary," Pat has written, "is a sanctuary for animals, not a zoo, and everything that is done is done with the animals' well-being and welfare placed at the highest level, and not for the pleasure of humans."

In his book, *A Different Nature: The Paradoxical World of Zoos and Their Uncertain Future*, David Hancocks asks that we consider the following questions in assessing whether animals living in zoos are being as well served as their human visitors.

Do the animals have the ability to get out of view of people if they so choose? Do they have space to get away from close proximity to visitors? Can they hide from other animals in their enclosures if they so choose? Do they have access to shady places in hot weather, warm spots on colder days? Are they able to enjoy distant views outside their enclosures? Is there a range of natural objects, materials, and vegetation to interact with? In short, do they have opportunities to carry out the important aspects of their natural lifestyles?

At the Wild Animal Sanctuary, the answer to every one of those questions is yes, yes, yes, yes, yes, yes, and YES!

Do animals have the ability to get out of view of people if they so choose? Do they have space to get away from close proximity to visitors? Can they hide from other animals in their enclosures if they so choose?

The Wild Animal Sanctuary provides its animal residents with ample opportunity to avoid their human observers, who are distant enough and far enough above ground on the elevated Mile into the Wild Walkway to be non-threatening. The habitats are enormous – ranging on average from five to twenty-five acres. Slight rises and ripples in the landscape, some natural, some created by Sanctuary operations staff provide respites and even microclimates for the residents. So, a grizzly or black bear or leopard or whoever can choose, on any given day, whether he or she is up to socializing with their habitat buddies. A family of exceedingly social African lions often congregates together. Less sociable tigers, who nonetheless agreeably share the same habitat, can choose to be as close to or as far from their "roommates" as they wish. Dens abound so an animal who wishes to get underground and out of sight can do so at will.

5.2 White tiger, Timara, in autumn

Do they have access to shady places in hot weather, warm spots on colder days?
Due to the lack of precipitation, short-grass prairie is not a biome with an abundance of trees. In truth, there are almost no trees, except for the hundreds planted by Sanctuary teams over the years. No rain equates to abundant sunshine and the eastern plains enjoy some three hundred sunny days a year. So, the Sanctuary team builds all manner of canopies, covers, and shade structures, which provide residents relief from the bright sun and summer heat. Some habitats extend under the broad trusses and metal platforms of the Walkway, which offers much sought after shade on hot sunny days. Plus, the carefully designed dens are cool in the summer and warm in the winter so they provide respite from whatever weather the Sanctuary may be experiencing.

5.3 Joker, an Arctic fox

On frigid winter days in Colorado, the sun can provide an unexpected amount of warmth. Plus, although we may think it is a cold day, the large carnivores may not. On a recent January morning when we volunteers were clad in heavy Sanctuary orange jackets, hats, and scarves, with hand warmers stuffed in our gloves, lions were stretched out in the snow, perhaps relishing the curious sensation of being warm on one side and cold on the other.

Are they able to enjoy distant views outside their enclosures?

If you want panoramic views and far-flung vistas, you could do no better than to spend time on Colorado's eastern plains. The distant views in the Sanctuary's prairie habitats extend as far as the eye can see to the horizon. Open fields surround its almost 800 acres. The Front Range of the Rockies can be seen rising in the distance seventy miles to the west. Pikes Peak is visible more than one hundred miles to the south. At the Sanctuary, the prairie landscape yields to big sky, which changes constantly. Flocks of gulls, starlings, and blackbirds soar and sweep overhead in summer. A solitary red-tailed hawk commandeers a telephone pole as a lookout for field mice. Bald eagles by the dozens sweep overhead in winter. For any species whose eyes are built for the long view, there could not be a better place than Colorado's expansive prairies.

Is there a range of natural objects, materials, and vegetation to interact with? In short, do they have opportunities to carry out the important aspects of their natural lifestyles?

Beyond the natural and man-made features in the landscape, each of the habitats has its "toys." Great empty cable spools are stacked in pyramids to provide elevated ledges for napping lions and tigers. Big cats sprawl on concrete "hammocks," tigers curl up on woven beds in the Tiger Roundhouse, lynx sleep high above the ground on multi-level platforms or curl up in stacked concrete pipes. Jaguars have access to a giant "jungle gym" and leopards lounge on their "sky bridge" platforms high above the prairie floor. For the bears, there are tire swings and massive fallen tree trunks for climbing. All the habitats have large stock tanks that are regularly filled with fresh water; some have large concrete pools complete with waterfalls, and yet others have expansive natural ponds with paddling ducks and croaking frogs.

Then there are the ever-busy bears. Bears are adept and lively explorers, wanderers, climbers, and diggers. They are genetically programmed to be on the move and when their movement is restricted, they become bored and often destructive. On a pleasant morning in mid-June, Tiny, a

5.4 This king of the beasts, and the cable spools, brings new meaning to the term "apex predator"

1,000-pound grizzly walks toward a sizable tractor tire, crawls inside, and flexes his jaw gently on the hard rubber edge. He endeavors to lift it with his front paws, then curls his great bulk into a comma inside the opening and rests his head on the rim. After a few minutes, he strolls across the compound toward the pool and waterfall. Folding his front feet under him he gently dips his nose into the cool water and drinks, breaking up bubbles and froth churned up by the waterfall. Sauntering slowly across the grass to the water tank, he heaves himself over the rim, splashes around a bit, and submerges everything except his head. A little while later, he leaves his cool bath, shakes the water off and wanders head down through the meadow, snuffling through the grass, pausing, chewing. Meanwhile, his roommate Natasha has been on her own trek around the habitat. Sometimes they meet up at the pool or in the water tank, splashing, jockeying for position, playing like two tykes in a plastic kiddie pool. Natasha likes to walk the double rim of the stock tank in a 360-degree circuit that would be the envy of any gymnast looking to master the balance beam. And so it goes. If the

5.5 Natasha and her stick

big cats sleep sixteen or eighteen hours a day, the bears forage for sixteen to eighteen hours each day. In answer to Hancocks' query, we would say yes, Sanctuary animals do "have opportunities to carry out the important aspects of their natural lifestyles."

At the Wild Animal Sanctuary the comfort and well-being of the animals always comes first. They are the residents; we are the guests. The Sanctuary welcomes with open arms the hundreds of thousands of people who walk through the Welcome Center every year. But it makes no promises that the animals will be entertaining, awake, or even visible to the visitors who have come into their home. That is what makes it a sanctuary.

There are thousands of animal sanctuaries and shelters across the United States and around the world. Most people are familiar with those that specialize in dogs and cats since just about every city and town in America has some type of rescue operation and protection for abandoned and abused family pets. Some sanctuaries specialize in horses and/or donkeys. Others take only wolves. Yet others focus on farm animals, birds, primates, or reptiles.

When, however, you start saving wild and dangerous large carnivores, a whole new set of challenges present themselves. The Wild Animal Sanctuary is hardly alone in its efforts to rescue, rehabilitate, and provide lifelong care for hundreds of such residents. Among the oldest large carnivore sanctuaries in the U.S. are: Big Cat Rescue Corporation in Tampa, Florida; Carolina Tiger Rescue in Pittsboro, North Carolina; Lions, Tigers, and Bears in San Diego, California; PAWS (Performing Animal Welfare Society) in Galt, California; Turpentine Creek Wildlife Refuge in Eureka Springs, Arkansas; and The Wildcat Sanctuary in Sandstone, Minnesota.

All are members of the Global Federation of Animal Sanctuaries (GFAS) and are required to comply with accreditation standards. While definitions may vary somewhat, a true animal sanctuary:

- Provides for high quality life-long care for its animals, including appropriate veterinary care
- Does not breed its animals
- Does not use or transport animals for any commercial use, including entertainment, exhibition, or commercial activities
- Does not buy, sell, trade or auction animals
- Prohibits direct contact between visitors and animals
- Upholds strong standards of animal care and complies with federal and state animal welfare laws and regulations
- Is a not-for-profit organization that meets appropriate ethical standards for development and fundraising

The best sanctuaries, Pat adds, "also go much further in providing large natural habitats for the animals and protecting them from any undue pressure from humans."

Unfortunately, the use of the term "sanctuary" does not guarantee that the high standards above will be met or maintained. Sadly, even sanctuaries with the best of intentions often struggle to preserve high, ethical standards of animal welfare and operations simply because it is so expensive to operate a well-run sanctuary. The Wild Animal Sanctuary has rescued animals from failing sanctuaries whose expenses have sky-rocketed, donations have plummeted, and animals have suffered for it.

What is even worse is the fact that any facility can call itself a "sanctuary." There is no shortage of commercial enterprises that abuse the privilege of calling themselves sanctuaries, as well as abusing the animals they own. So, it is up to the consumer to ferret out the bad operators and avoid or report them as circumstances dictate. One place to start is with the criteria above. The list clearly demonstrates that there is no room for roadside zoos, bear pits, cub pay-to-play and photo operations, or any type of outfit that uses exotic animals for entertainment or profit or allows human-animal contact. Plus, if you encounter a facility that calls itself a sanctuary and yet breeds its exotic animals, step away. It is not a sanctuary, it is a *scamtuary*.

The Wild Animal Sanctuary has led the way for forty years in not only meeting the requirements of animal welfare laws and complying with the criteria that define a true sanctuary – but in revamping existing laws and establishing new principles that adhere to a higher standard. Let's see how Pat and his team have done it.

Chapter 6

⠿ ⠿ ⠿ ⠿ ⠿ ⠿ ⠿ ⠿ ⠿ ⠿ ⠿ ⠿ ⠿ ⠿ ⠿ ⠿

Expansion and Education:
The Mission Goes Sky High

The Wild Animal Sanctuary has passed one milestone after another over the last forty years. The tiny enterprise that began with a jaguar cub named Freckles on Pat Craig's fifteen-acre family farm along Valmont Road moved to Lyons and grew to roughly forty furry residents in a little more than a decade. In 1994, when Pat moved the Sanctuary to 160 acres in Keenesburg, things began to grow exponentially. By 2010 the Sanctuary had grown to more than 220 animals in twenty habitats covering 240 acres. With the addition of 400 acres in June 2011 the land area more than doubled in size and at the end of 2012, more than 300 animals called the Sanctuary home. In 2018, having built out the acreage outside of Keenesburg and with no land available for purchase in the immediate area, the Sanctuary took the bold and unprecedented step of acquiring 9,684 acres in southeastern Colorado, thus creating The Wild Animal Refuge. Today, more than 500 animals live at the Sanctuary and Refuge including African lions, tigers, jaguars, leopards, black bears, grizzly bears, Asiatic black bears, Syrian brown bears, mountain lions, wolves, hyenas, African servals, bobcats, foxes, lynx, coyotes, and a variety of other exotic and domesticated animals such as coati mundi, kangaroos, wallabies, ostriches, emus, camels, alpacas, yaks, horses, and donkeys, not to mention an assortment of rescued dogs and cats. The story of The Wild Animal Sanctuary traverses a course from one tiny jaguar to the greatest sanctuary for large carnivores and other exotic animals in the world.

But the mission of the Sanctuary is not just to rescue exotic animals. What sets the Sanctuary apart are two things. The first is the ground-breaking, species-driven, and carefully tailored animal rehabilitation programs it has honed over the years and the life-long homes it provides the animals in its care. The second is its pivotal role in educating the public about the captive wildlife crisis. While Pat originally focused his energies on the daunting task of simply rescuing captive wildlife, he quickly came to recognize that in order for the animals to enjoy the comfort and freedom offered by the Sanctuary, most would require a nurturing, multifaceted healing process in order to fully recover from both the physical and psychological scars of neglect and abuse. It also became abundantly clear that if ever the numbers of captive wildlife around the world were to be reduced, it was critical to familiarize not only Coloradans but people across the country and around the world about the tragedy of captive wild animals. So, over the years, the mission of the Sanctuary has evolved to encompass rescue, rehabilitation and animal well-being, and public education. Education was given a big boost by a brilliant idea called The Mile into the Wild Walkway.

Visitors Flock to the Sanctuary

In the first half dozen years after relocating to Keenesburg, the Sanctuary was staffed by Pat, his son Casey Craig, an enthusiastic animal lover named Becca Miceli who would ultimately become the Sanctuary's Chief Science and Welfare Officer, and a small cadre of volunteers. It was not open to the public and Pat had no intention of encouraging curiosity seekers who wanted to see the large carnivores under his loving care. Nonetheless, occasionally people would call ahead to ask if they could stop by and look at the animals. Some would not even bother to call; they would simply show up, having heard about this amazing place on the prairie that was home to big cats and bears. "We had a dirt parking lot and the County Road was dirt, the road in from the gate was dirt," Pat reminisces, "We would be working and cleaning. People would show up and you'd answer a couple of questions and you'd keep doing your work...People kept saying I want to leave a donation. We'd say, okay just leave it down under that rock. We finally put up a table with a flyer and a rock." Yet, even with a small number of visitors straggling over the Sanctuary's doorstep, Pat could tell that the animals were uncomfortable. They would tense up, wary of seeing strangers invading their territories, and would steal away to their favorite hiding places until the invaders were gone. Their uneasiness deepened Pat's conviction that his instincts were right; there was no room for the public at the Sanctuary.

Yet, members of the Sanctuary Board of Directors, volunteers, visitors, and even some friends would repeatedly tell him what a special place the Sanctuary was – and one that should be shared with others. "Open the Sanctuary to the public!" they would implore. Pat would have none of it. He had long argued three points: The Sanctuary was built for the animals; visitors stressed out the animals; therefore, there was no way he was going to encourage more visitors to come to the Sanctuary. Period. The problem was visitors had not gotten the memo on this one. They just kept showing up. Their numbers kept climbing as word began to trickle out about the tigers, lions, jaguars, bears, and wolves living outside of Keenesburg. Then visitors began asking if they could buy a soda or a snack. A visitor with diabetes was not feeling well and needed something to eat; Pat ran back to the house and grabbed a package of peanuts for the ailing guest. Some asked if there were T-shirts for sale. Others suggested he print and sell baseball caps. Interest was on the rise and visitors kept on coming.

Unfortunately, the captive wildlife crisis was intensifying too. Even worse, too few people even knew there was a captive wildlife crisis. It became clear to Pat, his closest advisors, and the people who worked and volunteered at The Wild Animal Sanctuary that, if the ultimate goal was to crack the captive wildlife crisis, it was critical to "reach as many people as possible…educate them about the problems surrounding captive wildlife… and then work together to end the abuse." Education was the key. The issue was, how to educate the public in a way that was cost effective and efficient without compromising the well-being of the animals. Pat was often invited to speak to small community groups and school classes about the problem and the Sanctuary's commitment to solving it. But with only a few talks a month, it was clear to Pat that "it would take decades for us to reach just a tiny portion of Colorado's population – let alone have any kind of impact on a national level." Plus, there were just not enough hours in a day. He recalls, "Creating opportunities to speak with the public was difficult due to a number of factors, but the biggest issue was time…We still had a Sanctuary to run, and needed to find a way to continue caring for the animals – while also educating people on a daily basis." It was becoming more obvious that educating the public on any kind of large scale would mean opening the Sanctuary to the public.

But what would that mean to the animals who relished the safety of the large fenced habitats and the freedom to move about without worry or trauma? They had had enough suffering in their lives. This was their forever home. And now it would be open to intruders.

Pat hit upon the solution that would be ideal for his animal residents, and, as it turned out, for visitors, too. He agreed to open the Sanctuary to the public – but only if visitors would be confined to observation areas elevated well above the habitats. He recalls with a smile, "that really blew people's minds. Nobody could fathom what it was going to look like. I had to draw it out on a piece of paper with the ramp and the poles. I had to sketch it for people to even get it. Even so, most people didn't grasp it until it was built." Even some of those who had been advocating for a more public role considered the idea odd if not outrageous; others could not quite figure out why an elevated walkway was even necessary. That is because none of them, save Pat, had been there some twenty years before when it was time to put a roof on a storage shed at the family farm.

About a year after Pat started working with large carnivores, he came to the sudden realization that tigers, lions, bears, jaguars, and similar predators do not consider the sky to be part of their territory. He had spent more than a year getting to know his new charges, maintaining as stable and tranquil an environment as possible, essentially tiptoeing around his sizable occupants so as not to startle or scare them. As the number of wild animals increased, so did the need for food and supplies. It was time to build a small storage building immediately adjacent to the carnivore compound. He began constructing the building, doing as much as possible at some distance from their enclosures and being careful not to cause too much commotion. But one morning he had to work on the metal roof and was concerned about how the animals were going to react to the whine of a circular saw and the constant banging of a hammer on steel. He remembers thinking, "How do I do this with those guys right there?" Without any viable alternative, he took his first tentative steps toward an experiment that would later change the course of the Sanctuary – and of his life.

> So, I got up on the roof. They didn't care that I got on the roof. I started banging and watching them just to see their reactions, and nothing. I thought, really? I ran a power saw, and nothing. Somebody looking my way might continue looking, but they never went, whoa, what's that? Or get up and move over in their cage. I thought, this is really weird. This would scare most people. The horses would run away. But the carnivores were not showing any sign that the noise had any impact.

Indeed, it was clear that the animals were unaffected by the presence of a human directly above them nor did they seem to care that the human was making a lot of noise. They clearly had no fear of people walking and working over their heads. In fact, they did not even have any *interest* in people walking and working over their heads. Pat likens it to the way we humans react upon spotting an airplane flying thousands of feet above us. Truth is, we do not react at all. So it was for the animals with Pat rattling about on the storage shed roof above them. Satisfied that his work would not bother the next-door neighbors, so to speak, Pat sawed and banged on the structure until the storage shed was finished.

Sometime later he renovated the adjacent barn and made it into an apartment with a second story window from which he could observe the animals both day and night. Again, they paid no attention to the person gazing at them from fifteen feet above their heads. The roof, the apartment window, and other similar circumstances convinced Pat that large carnivore territory was planted firmly on the ground. The sky was inconsequential to how they perceived their world and how they established personal boundaries. Filed away as one more step along the large-carnivore learning curve, these experiences ultimately planted the seed of an idea that would sprout and become the Mile into the Wild Walkway.

The concept of an elevated walkway and observation decks was brilliant. Getting visitors above ground level would enable the animals to go about their daily business without feeling their homes had been invaded, thus eliminating the stressors that lead to stereotypic behaviors. Having visitors well over the animals' heads would be like Pat building the roof on the storage shed, only without power saws and hammers. It would allow the Sanctuary to welcome visitors for the first time, strengthening its mission to educate the public about the captive wildlife crisis. Not only that, visitors would enjoy a much better view of the Sanctuary's residents in their large multi-acre habitats than they ever would have experienced at ground level. It was the beginning of a new era in large carnivore education for The Wild Animal Sanctuary. Pat explains: "By utilizing an elevated system of observation decks and walkways, it was now possible for us to educate the public about our work relating to the captive wildlife crisis, while also guaranteeing the animals we rescued would be able to continue to enjoy their newly enriched lives here at the Sanctuary." Visitors would become part of the sky. The land-based territories of the big cats and bears would be undisturbed. The animals would still come first.

Like pretty much everything else at The Wild Animal Sanctuary, it seems the tiny seed planted in Pat Craig's mind when he was building the roof of the storage shed grew organically over the years into a unique and award-winning initiative. Planted, nurtured, and watered, the seed ultimately germinated into an elevated footbridge anchored by an enormous Welcome Center at one end and a large snack bar and rest area at the other, with the Bear Deck and the Lion House in between. There was no grand plan. No detailed blueprint. No consultants or contractors called in. Just a kernel of an idea that grew to meet the needs at the time.

The seed sprouted at the southeast corner of the property where Pat had built the original circular animal compound with pie-shaped enclosures. Although it would later become known as the Tiger Roundhouse and be dedicated solely to that species, at this point a variety of animals lived there. Here, where visitors would wander in and place their donations under the rock on the table, staff and volunteers began building the first observation platforms in 2002. First, the Sanctuary team built a ramp up to an observation area above the Roundhouse. Then they crafted a large viewing platform, christened the Lion Deck, just beyond the ramp. From the Lion Deck visitors could see not only lions but tigers, bears, and other residents in the surrounding habitats.

In 2003, for the first time in its history and with little fanfare, the Sanctuary opened to visitors on the weekends. The floodgates were set ajar. As the crowds continued to flow in, the Sanctuary opened the original Welcome Center in 2005 (now the snack bar just east of the Tiger Roundhouse), built partially with materials donated from the massive Interstate-25 and light rail Transportation Expansion Project, famously known in Denver and along the Front Range as the "T-Rex" Project. In 2006, the team completed a 2,500 square foot observation deck on top of the (old) Welcome Center so people could better see the grizzlies to the north and the wolves to the east.

The number of visitors, which had started as a trickle became a steady stream, and by 2010 the Sanctuary was welcoming more than 50,000 visitors a year.

In early 2011 the rescue of the twenty-five lions from Bolivia, the construction of their Lion House, and the widespread media coverage that accompanied them to the Sanctuary ratcheted visitor numbers up to nearly 100,000. With more Sanctuary habitats being built to the north, it was becoming clear that the existing elevated structures were inadequate both to handle the number of visitors and to allow them to see many of its residents.

6.1 Early visitors on the Lion Deck

It was time to build the Mile into the Wild Walkway. Pat, Casey, and the team turned their attention to two challenges. How to build it. And where to put it.

6.2 The Wild Animal Sanctuary prior to building the Walkway with the Tiger Roundhouse left of center and the angled Welcome Center to the right.

Above it All: The Mile into the Wild Walkway

American architect Frank Lloyd Wright would have appreciated the resourcefulness of Pat and Casey's approach to constructing a pioneering walkway twenty-five feet (or more) above the prairie floor. In 1933 Wright designed the Johnson Wax building in Racine, Wisconsin with what he dubbed his "lily pad" columns. At nine-inches in diameter at the base, the implausibly thin, steel-reinforced columns rose twenty-one feet, flared gently to eighteen inches at the top, and then puddled into 18.5 foot diameter circular platforms that supported the roof. Engineers were rightly skeptical and building code inspectors refused to approve the design, demanding that the architect load a test column with twelve tons of concrete in a rigorous test of strength. Wright agreed. Then the famously self-confident architect kept loading the top of the test column with more and more tonnage until finally, at sixty tons of concrete – five times the amount required by building code officials – the lily pad column collapsed. Wright was granted his building permit.

Although they may not have been familiar with Wright's engineering triumph in Racine, we would suggest Pat and Casey used a similar testing strategy on the walkway, and then, for good measure, topped the architect by driving a van on top of it. The idea was to build the wood and steel framework in forty-foot sections supported by enormous trusses equipped to handle the high winds that scour the prairie. They built a test section and then loaded it up with more than six tons of concrete. The railing deflected less than a quarter of an inch. Then they drove one of their Ford vans on it. All good. The engineers gave it a thumbs up. In fact, they determined that a 10,000 pound vehicle doing sixty miles an hour and then slamming on the brakes would rack the structure less than an inch. Pat and Casey got their building permit.

6.3 Building the Walkway in forty-foot sections

That is also when Ryan Clements got his first job at the Sanctuary. Ryan had been working at one of Colorado's premier ski resorts for more than a decade, but he felt that something was missing. He began driving down from the mountains on the weekends just to volunteer at The Wild Animal Sanctuary. One day Casey spied Ryan's welding truck and asked who the welder was. When Casey found Ryan, he offered him a job; the Walkway was just getting started and there would be no shortage of welding skills needed to put it together. Ryan's response? "Yes!" He grins, "I went back to the mountains and gave my two weeks' notice. I had been there fourteen years...But that is not what I wanted...I never once asked Casey what I was getting paid. I was like, yes, I'm in."

The team determined that the Walkway would head due west from the Lion Deck, make a sharp right turn at the intersection of bear, tiger, and lion habitats, and head north to a new Bear Deck and onto the Lion House that had been constructed earlier that year. By the summer of 2011, construction on the eight-foot wide Walkway was well underway. The 4,800-foot long footbridge ultimately extended from the Roundhouse all the way to the observation deck of the Lion House in the spring of 2012. A new entrance and additional parking near the Bear Deck accommodated the visitors that kept pouring in and who could now stroll almost a mile along the Walkway above massive habitats housing grizzly bears, tigers, wolves, and, of course, lions.

6.4 The new Walkway looking toward the Lion House on the left and the Tiger Roundhouse on the right

A few short years later with the number of visitors climbing fast and a renewed commitment to public education, the team decided to move the visitor entrance to the extreme northwest corner of the property. Parking had become increasingly congested and the sheer number of visitors was overwhelming the capacity of the original entrance. The Sanctuary determined to build and open a new 48,000 square foot Welcome Center at the north end of the property and turn the original Welcome Center into a snack bar and rest area. The new 160-foot by 300-foot ClearSpan structure would house reception areas, large and small meeting rooms, a café, an ice cream shop, a gift shop, and various staff offices. A grand staircase and a series of handicap accessible ramps would get visitors from the ground floor to a new section of walkway that would connect the Welcome Center to the Lion House. The plan was ambitious, and it came to fruition when the new Welcome Center and the final stretch of the Walkway opened in the fall of 2016.

In fact, the Mile into the Wild Walkway exceeded all expectations given that the completed structure was, in fact, well over a mile. "As most Sanctuary supporters know," Pat wrote, "we have gone to great lengths to build our system of elevated walkways and decks for the benefit of the animals we rescue." The words "great lengths" proved to be rather prophetic. In October 2016, much to everyone's delight, Guinness World Records issued a certificate to the Sanctuary for having the longest elevated footbridge in the world. At 7,972 feet or 1.51 miles from the Welcome Center to the Tiger Roundhouse, the Walkway surpassed a footbridge ninety

6.5 The new Welcome Center

miles north of New York City that crosses the Hudson River and so earned the Guinness honor.

Today, more than 200,000 visitors a year enter the new Welcome Center. First-timers – as well as frequent supporters who continue to be enthralled by the Sanctuary's mission – watch a short orientation video played on a twelve by twenty foot wall of ultra-high definition video screens. It introduces the important work of the Sanctuary in the context of the captive wildlife crisis and familiarizes onlookers with the rescue and rehabilitation stories of some of the animals who live there. The video was our first remarkable introduction to The Wild Animal Sanctuary, and it is an introduction we share with family and friends who accompany us on frequent visits there. The Welcome Center space is bright and cheerful with people milling about, making their way to and from the Walkway, and staff and volunteers standing out in brilliant orange as they hustle from one project or assignment to another.

The Mile into the Wild Walkway was a master stroke. Without it, Pat would never have allowed the number of visitors seen today onto the grounds. Moreover, the educational mission of the Sanctuary would never have been realized, and ongoing future opportunities to continue to raise awareness of the captive wildlife crisis would have been lost. Pat has written:

> Our elevated walkways and decks are the answer to keeping the unique peace and tranquility alive, as the absence of people – or better yet – threats to their territory at ground level is the key ingredient for success...Visitors are able to see the animals enjoying the same expanse, beauty, and overall peaceful setting that is the Sanctuary, while both they and the animals below remain separated by an invisible barrier that guarantees happy outcomes for all.

In the fall of 2019, GFAS agreed. The accrediting body had for years refused to grant accreditation to The Wild Animal Sanctuary because it failed to meet the GFAS criteria for guided tours. GFAS policies specifically state: "No tours allowed that are not guided and conducted in a careful manner that minimizes the impact on the animals and their environment, does not cause them stress, and gives them the ability to seek undisturbed privacy and quiet." The Wild Animal Sanctuary had never had to offer guided tours because visitors could independently stroll along the elevated

Walkway at their own pace and leisure. Of course, the Walkway from its inception was designed to minimize "the impact on the animals and their environment," eliminate "stress," and enable the animals to "seek undisturbed privacy and quiet." But the accrediting body stuck to its guns: no guided tours, no accreditation – until Pat persuaded an accrediting team to come and see the Sanctuary for itself in the fall of 2019. Only then did GFAS fully appreciate the value of the elevated Walkway to the animals who lived there. As a result, GFAS changed its guided tour criteria for the Sanctuary and granted it full accreditation. Once again, Pat had changed the captive wildlife paradigm.

Strolling the Mile into the Wild Walkway is like traversing a timeline of the history of The Wild Animal Sanctuary. Starting at the new Welcome Center deck at the top of the grand staircase, the visitor first walks *back* in time past the newer leopard and jaguar habitats, past numerous lion habitats and through the Lion House, to the Bear Deck, over the original entrance drive, left at the corner and on to what is now the Tiger Roundhouse and the snack bar and rest area that served as the original entrance to the Sanctuary. Turning around, visitors then walk *into* the future from the place where it all started, making their way to the enormous new Welcome Center where the first thing they see is a flat screen highlighting the features and future of The Wild Animal Refuge – a key harbinger of what is to come.

Chapter 7

●: ●: ●: ●: ●: ●: ●: ●: ●: ●: ●: ●: ●: ●: ●: ●: ●:
●: ●: ●: ●: ●: ●: ●: ●: ●: ●: ●: ●: ●: ●: ●: ●: ●:

When You've Seen One Rescue…
You've Seen One Rescue

African lions Masai, Dante, and Mara came out of the California film industry. Mountain lions CeCe and Felix arrived from an amusement park in Florida. The tiger named Chase came from a private home in Missouri. Clay, Daniel, Enzo, and Thomas were among the thirty-nine tigers rescued from Joe Exotic's tiger breeding operation in Oklahoma. Lioness Lacey and her children Sampson and Tabitha, as documented in the 2010 film *The Elephant in the Living Room*, hailed from Ohio. Marley, a grizzly bear, came to the Sanctuary from Georgia. A bobcat named Shadow was rescued from a shopping mall exhibit in Des Moines, Iowa, as were wolves Keona, Raven, and Yukon and foxes Granite, Marble, Kit, and Red. Sierra, a tiger from Illinois, was owned by a Chicago gang member. The grizzly bear dubbed Trouble arrived from Alaska via Duluth, Minnesota. With this brief but representative list, we have barely covered the extent and reach of the captive wildlife crisis in America.

Indeed, the geographic scope of four decades of Sanctuary rescues is a telling and dismal barometer of the problem. Over the years, PETA, the Humane Society of the U.S. (HSUS), state attorneys general, the U.S. Fish and Wildlife Service (USFWS), Tigers in America (TIA), and many similar wild animal welfare and legal defense organizations, as well private citizens, have called upon the Sanctuary to rescue animals from across the United States. In responding to these appeals, the Sanctuary has rescued animals from almost every state in the union.

While a historically large number of rescues in states such as California, Ohio, and Texas may be indicative of lenient state laws or poorly enforced regulations, they also reflect what happens when stricter exotic animal laws are passed at the state level. New laws force commercial enterprises and private owners to surrender their animals, creating a flurry of urgent rescues in a short period of time. Some state numbers also are higher due to a disproportionate number of rescues involving large quantities of animals there. As examples, besides the Oklahoma tigers from the Wynnewood Exotic Animal Park, three of the Sanctuary's largest rescues have included twenty-five bears from San Antonio; seventeen bears from Helen, Georgia; and a dozen tigers and leopards from a "scamtuary" in California.

Most of the animals at the Sanctuary are law enforcement confiscations. Some have been seized in no-knock raids. Others have been rescued under the protection of armed law enforcement officers. More than a few have arrived at the Sanctuary as wards of the court. These confiscated animals are the unlucky victims of legal battles between law-breaking owners who want their animals back and government regulators bent on not letting that happen. Animals also come from other legitimate sanctuaries who lack the space or resources to take in additional animals and call Pat Craig asking if he has room for just a few more. Some animals come from sanctuaries that are failing financially. Regardless of the best of altruistic intentions, it is enormously expensive to run a well-managed wildlife sanctuary. The worst of these are sanctuaries that have been taken over by federal or state agencies after they repeatedly failed routine animal welfare inspections.

Easier adoptions come from zoo "transplants" and private owners who voluntarily surrender their exotic animals. Public zoos may need to rehome certain animals because the facility has run out of room or is eliminating or reallocating exhibits. Voluntary surrenders by private owners generally arise from genuine concerns about personal safety or as the consequence of a relocation. Some animals have been given to the Sanctuary by families who moved to Colorado with, say, their pet fox only to learn that exotic animal ownership is illegal here. Those surrenders often involve smaller carnivores such as foxes, bobcats, or African servals.

Regardless of the call that comes into Pat, the Sanctuary is always at the ready to respond. The team will go anywhere, anyway, anytime to rescue animals in need. The large rescues are mind-boggling. It takes a tremendous amount of know-how to safely load and transport forty-two large carnivores almost 700 miles from Wynnewood, Oklahoma to Keenesburg, Colorado. But the team also has driven 1,500 miles or more to collect a single animal. In fact, Sanctuary rescue trucks and trailers have logged millions of miles on rescue missions across the United States.

Although you might think that a rescue commences when staff leap into the transport vehicles and race out the drive and onto the highway, the first step is to confirm that the animal is the right fit for the Sanctuary. The Sanctuary gives priority to animals who have nowhere else to go. In order to achieve that aim, Pat is deeply saddened but prepared to say "no" when there are other rehoming possibilities for the animal in question (as evidenced by the fact that historically about fifty percent of rescue calls have had to be declined) and when saying "yes" would compromise the resources and financial health of his own organization – and thus, all the animals currently in his care. It is not just a matter of going on a rescue. Based on the number of calls that come in, the Sanctuary could probably go on a rescue almost every day. Instead, careful thought goes into accepting an animal, ensuring that the newcomer will be afforded a forever home and the best quality of life possible. If Pat believes the Sanctuary can do that, the rescue gets the go ahead.

Rescuing a large carnivore, however, is not just a matter of driving the trailer to a roadside zoo or some other venue, ushering the animal into a transport cage, and driving home. It is an operation requiring a tremendous amount of coordination and planning. Multiply that times seventeen bears, or thirty-nine tigers and you get a sense of the challenges that accompany the business of wildlife rescues. The logistics team convenes to work out the details. As Pat related to us, "Casey and Becca and I discuss the operation…Becca takes care of prepping for the animals. She will talk to the animal caretakers and the med staff about the condition of the animals and getting habitats and dens ready. Casey and Ryan take care of the equipment. They will make sure the vehicles are in tip-top shape, have been serviced, and are ready to go."

Every rescue is unique, but all Sanctuary rescues require four things: transportation, equipment and supplies, personnel, and paperwork. Over the years the Sanctuary has acquired a fleet of distinct, specially-equipped transport vehicles to accommodate rescues both large and small, and animals of all shapes and sizes. Everything from two-horse trailers to custom-built rigs are lined up behind the Carnivore Nutrition Center. With their sleek design, relatively low profiles, and lightweight, fuel-saving aluminum bodies, the enclosed, gooseneck trailers are the most impressive. Each of the three forty-foot long trailers is hauled by a beefy Dodge 5500 truck that can handle the tonnage of seven to nine transport cages filled with big cats and bears. The cages are secured to rails on one side of the trailer, leaving an aisle along the opposite side so animal caregivers can check on their charges at periodic rest stops.

7.1 Pint-size rescued Maltese dog Marcel demonstrating the substantial size of the Sanctuary's transport cages

Of course, a rescue involves a lot more than transport vehicles and transport cages. The vehicles are equipped with everything from welders to extension cords to jacks, hydraulic power units, generators, and winches that run on small gas engines in the event electrical power is unavailable. As Pat says, "we try to go prepared for anything – trailers breaking down or getting to the site and having to winch a cage up over a twelve foot wall. We have a lot of equipment we don't necessarily break out every time, but it goes on every rescue." The medical gear and pharmaceutical stores taken for the animals are equally substantial. Sedation medications and the darts and guns needed to dispense them are always on board, as are emergency first aid kits, oxygen tanks, intravenous fluids, medications for injuries, and other similar supplies.

Specially trained staff must always be at the ready to move large carnivores across the country – and the world. When Pat says "yes" to the rescue, the team is assembled and on call. Kent Drotar remembers, "I went on the rescue to Ohio for Timara the white tiger, Montana the mountain lion, and Jumanji the black leopard. They called us on Thursday night and said we need you to be at this place on Saturday morning. We had thirty-six hours to get ready and get there."

The amount of manpower needed is one of the biggest decisions in a rescue. Rescues vary from one or two people to a dozen or even more. If the

Sanctuary can rent a Telehandler, a type of four-wheel drive forklift with a telescoping crane, and have it delivered in advance to the site, a large team may not be necessary. Pat explains:

> We go to so many of these facilities where the ground is wet and trying to roll a cage that weighs 800 pounds where the four wheels dig in is almost impossible. Casey and I fought that for so many years, pushing cages through quagmires. In the last few years instead of taking tons of muscle with us, we have a forklift delivered. We pull our cages out of the trailer and drive them over with the forklift without dragging them through wet dirt and mud. Once the cats or bears are inside, we pick them up with the forklift and drive them back to the trailer where we reach out and stick the cage in without even having to use the ramp.

But in contentious rescues where the owner of the animals has no interest in cooperating by allowing equipment to be delivered beforehand, or those where the terrain is unable to accommodate a Telehandler, this rental option may be off the table. So, a larger number of people are needed to move animals. Turnaround time also affects team size: the smaller the window of opportunity to load the animals, the greater the size of the team.

In the fall of 2017 the Sanctuary embarked on its first rescue of nineteen tigers at Joe Exotic's zoo in Wynnewood, Oklahoma, some time before Joe's conviction. Pat took a dozen people with him:

> The reason we took an "army" to Joe's is that he stipulated we couldn't come in before 7:00 a.m. and we had to be out by 9:00 a.m. So we had two hours to try to move nineteen animals the first time and twenty the second time…We knew we were going to have to sedate the animals to move them, so we took the vets, Val and Felicia. Sedating five or six animals is hard enough, let alone nineteen in two hours. There's nobody on the planet that could do that besides us.

The rescue team often expands at the site with the addition of PETA or other officials and with the protection of private security or law enforcement. In some cases, a law enforcement unit goes in first to secure the site and placate angry owners. Often, just the presence of security or police will be enough to stabilize the situation and let Sanctuary staff quietly and efficiently get on with their work. Such was the case in the Joe Exotic rescue, where PETA had hired private security in advance. Pat remembers arriving the first morning:

Everybody at Joe's wore a gun. PETA had told us the court said Joe was not allowed to be on site. But I didn't believe it. I told PETA, "I guarantee you Joe will be there. Joe has to be the star of everything. He will be there." Sure enough we pull in and he's standing there in the parking lot. He's the first guy we meet. I said all it takes is for Joe to get mad and blow his lid and all of a sudden a shot is going to ring out from one of the guys who works for him and it's going to become the shootout at the OK Corral.

Fortunately, calmer heads prevailed. The Sanctuary sedated the animals and was out the door as required. The tigers and bears arrived safely in Colorado to enjoy new freedom on the plains.

Finally, there is the most mundane but not the least important part of a rescue: the paperwork. Without the paperwork, the rescue team may as well stay home because the rescue will, literally, go nowhere. To bring an exotic animal into Colorado, the Sanctuary first needs permission from Colorado Parks and Wildlife (CPW); once approved, the permitting request goes to the Colorado Department of Agriculture. Permit applications detail the species, gender, date of birth, background and history, purchase and transfer history, and current health. The paperwork does not stop with Colorado. For states such as Kentucky and Wyoming, permits are required to even drive wild animals into and through the state. International paperwork is more daunting, filling a binder with a dozen tabs and pages upon pages of documentation. Pat admits that everyone thinks a sanctuary director stays above the everyday, mundane operations, but "ninety percent of my job is on the back side doing all the paperwork and complicated permits."

Even though all rescues have in common the careful coordination of transportation, equipment and supplies, personnel, and paperwork processing, every animal comes with a unique story – and its rescue by the Sanctuary is an important part of its story. With more than a thousand animals rescued in the past forty years, it is impossible to do them all justice. So, with our apologies to those who have been excluded from these pages but are never overlooked by Sanctuary staff, here are a few rescue stories, first, from across the United States – and then, from around the world.

Black Forest Bear "Pit" is More Like It

It is striking how many urgent rescues seem to take place just as the holiday season is gearing up. As if things were not crazy enough during the month of December, agreeing to rescue eighteen grizzlies and black bears from the Black Forest Bear Park in Georgia was surely going to add to the insanity. In December of 2013 Pat learned from PETA that the Park was closing for good because the bank was about to foreclose on the perennially delinquent mortgage – and it wanted the bears out.

There are few facilities in the country willing and able to take that many bears, let alone that many at once. As Brittany Peet from the PETA Foundation shared with us, "Placing bears is really difficult. They are so long lived and so expensive to take care of because they eat so much produce…and they are destructive. They can easily destroy a habitat with a slap of their paw…But the Sanctuary is always willing to go the literal extra mile and do whatever it takes to help animals who need to be rescued." Such was the case here.

The Black Forest Bear Park had been confining black and grizzly bears, not in lush forested surroundings as the name would suggest, but in deep concrete bunkers for years. Even worse, the bears were allowed to breed each year. When new cubs are born each year at bear-breeding outfits, the staff routinely pulls the youngsters from their mothers within days or weeks of their birth and hand-feeds them. The orphaned cubs are put on display for the viewing pleasure of visiting tourists. When the cubs get too big to elicit the oohs and ahs of adoring but unthinking crowds, they are sold to other exotic animal venues.

7.2 Bears in bunkers at the Black Forest Bear Park

7.3 Bear in a cage at the Black Forest Bear Park

The attachment between a mother bear and her cubs is legendary; there is hardly a crueler act than separating them. Unlike tigers whose mothers will leave their young in the den while they hunt for food to bring back to the brood, bear cubs are *never* away from their mother. In the wild, cubs are born during the winter and when it is time to leave the den in the spring, the new family troops out together. Where the mother goes, so go the cubs, foraging for food, absorbing territory boundaries, and learning the basics of bear wilderness survival. The nurturing mother bear and her cubs are together every hour of every day for two years or even longer. There is no fluffier, bulkier, or fiercer 24/7 security blanket than a Mama Bear. As heartbreaking as it must have been for the mothers to be repeatedly separated from their cubs at the Bear Park after nursing them all winter, it would have been worse for the cubs. As Pat has noted, "Bear cubs are not genetically programmed to be left alone for even one second, let alone hours on end. Orphaned bear cubs…absolutely panic when they are left alone or lose sight of their mothers." These cubs experience the most severe separation anxiety, crying out for their mothers and licking their paws or sucking on the ears of littermates to soothe themselves and their siblings.

Shuttering the Black Forest Bear Park was the best thing that could have happened to the bears; the even better thing was being rescued by The Wild Animal Sanctuary. Staff and volunteers got busy converting forty-five acres of raw land into three new fifteen-acre habitats with underground dens, ponds, and water tanks. Pat got going on the paperwork necessary to transport the bears across state lines from the East Coast to the Rockies. Finally, the team focused on preparing three of the Sanctuary's large rescue rigs and eighteen transport cages for a late-December trek to Georgia. Then word came from PETA that O.B. and Ursula, two female grizzly bears, had been bred last spring and were probably pregnant, with the babies due in early to mid-January. That is when things really got busy.

You might be asking yourself, as we did, why two mother bears bred at least nine months ago had not yet given birth. The gestation period for bears is only about two months but the timing is affected by delayed implantation and hibernation. Bears mate during the late spring or summer, but the fertilized eggs do not implant in the female's womb until around November just when it is time to hibernate. Hibernation is commonly associated with winter survival, but it is also essential to reproduction. If the mother bear does not consume enough calories during the summer and fall to sustain fetal growth, or she is not able to hibernate, the eggs will spontaneously abort. Without a hibernation period in the winter, there will be no cubs emerging in the spring. Bear cubs are born during hibernation in January or February. Generally, anywhere from one to three tiny, one-pound cubs (blind, hairless, and toothless!) thrive on their mother's milk, gaining perhaps fifteen pounds over the roughly four-month hibernation period while winter rages on. It is a quite implausible and completely remarkable reproductive feat.

Pat and the rescue team realized it would be inhumane to move the possibly expectant mothers cross-country to brand new surroundings in late December within a week or two of their deliveries. The "animals-first" motto was once again put into action and the rescue team decided to go get the pregnant bears immediately. A team left Keenesburg on the twenty-two hour drive to Georgia, loaded up the two expectant mothers and turned the rig around for home. They also brought with them four bear cubs, all under two years of age, who had long been separated from their mothers. The new groups comfortably settled into enclosures recently vacated by other bears who had been moved to different habitats.

When an Arctic blast delayed habitat construction at the Sanctuary the bank acquiesced on its eviction stance and plans to collect the remaining bears were pushed to the second week of January. By early 2014 the remaining twenty-two hour, non-stop trips to and from Georgia had been completed and the newly rescued bears (now totaling seventeen because, sadly, one of the bears had died) were released into their new homes. Over the next few weeks as hibernation instincts started to kick in, they began disappearing one by one into their cozy underground dens.

Over the course of the winter, the animal care staff wondered if O.B. and Ursula were actually pregnant. They also worried. Would the mother bears nurture or abandon their cubs? Although the owner at the bear park had repeatedly bred his female bears, they never had to rear cubs as they would have in the wild. When Ursula and O.B., with three cubs each, surfaced from their dens in the spring, instinct kicked in and both Mama Bears proved worthy of the task at hand. The staff christened O.B.'s cubs Helen, George, and Mel and Ursula's cubs Sam, Anna, and Alex. As the days grew longer the mothers and cubs materialized more frequently until the cubs were soon dashing and gamboling about. Today, the cubs are grown, but the families still live together.

7.4 Ursula and her new cubs

When Sanctuaries Fail: The Demise of the Spirit of the Hills Wildlife Sanctuary

After a September 2016 review of the Spirit of the Hills Wildlife Sanctuary in Spearfish, South Dakota, the Animal and Plant Health Inspection Service (APHIS) issued a grim report. Sick and aging animals were not getting proper medications. Veterinarians had not been called in to care for animals clearly in need. An animal deemed "low maintenance" was only given food and water every three days or so. Animal records were missing or incomplete. Cages and enclosures were not properly cleaned and sanitized; animal facilities were strewn with feces and urine, accumulated trash, junk, plywood, sharp wires, and other discarded and dangerous materials. Food was contaminated and stored in areas infested with flies and vermin.

The sanctuary was clearly in trouble. Volunteers conceded that feeding protocols were not being followed. Although animal keepers had long been adhering to established routines, the director of Spirit of the Hills had forbidden anyone else to feed the animals some months before. He alone began taking care of this crucial – and time consuming – task, raising the question of whether animals were being properly fed. Although the director originally resisted USDA confiscation of his animals, once the USDA team was on site, he suddenly changed his mind and agreed to voluntarily surrender all animals to the government officials. Later that night, inexplicably leaving his residence around midnight to purportedly administer medications to a tiger, he entered an adjacent tiger's cage and was mauled. Sheriff's Deputies shot and killed the tiger and took the director to a nearby hospital to have his wounds treated; he was later released.

When contacted by the USDA, Pat had agreed to take about a dozen animals straightaway, and another half dozen or so at a future date. Having spent the previous night at a nearby hotel, the Sanctuary team was ready to begin the rescue operations bright and early when USDA officials called Pat to apprise him of the midnight tiger attack. Even with Spirit of the Hills swarming with USDA officials and police, the rescue went forward as planned.

Spirit of the Hills was located on the northern edge of the Black Hills National Forest, just south of the town of Spearfish. The rugged and forested terrain could not have been more challenging. Animal enclosures had been constructed haphazardly and connected by narrow trails that provided little or no access to the enclosures. Pat split his team of six into three groups to assess the animals and formulate a logistics plan for the day.

Between the steep grades, tight corridors, irregular surfaces and overall lack of road base, every animal transfer was like pulling teeth...Hour after hour our three teams constantly split apart and reconvened...Some animals, like the black bears, required our team members to carry their lightly-sedated, but also extremely large, bodies up a steep grade leading to an enclosure doorway. Huffing and puffing, our crew made the first few trips without having to stop...but even the fittest members of the group rejoiced when a 30-second pit stop was made.

By the end of a long and grueling day, two things had happened. The three Sanctuary trailers, carrying seven bears, ten big cats, and one wolf were on the road bound for Colorado and the Spirit of the Hills Board of Directors agreed to surrender the sanctuary's license to the USDA. With the Board's decision, there were suddenly more animals to be rescued, so one of the teams unloaded in Keenesburg and then headed back to South Dakota to pick up four more bears and two wolves.

7.5 Eli Hollister, Casey Craig, and Ryan Clements hauling a gurney with a black bear to a transport crate

7.6 Becca Miceli administering fluids to a sedated bear

While Pat despairs that he cannot say "yes" to all the rescues about which he is contacted, he also maintains that being unable to say "no" is what gets an animal sanctuary in trouble. That is what happened to Spirit of the Hills. Started in 1999, it had at one point grown to more than 320 animals and forty different species – not only large and small carnivores, but birds, cats, dogs, squirrels, pigs, sheep, and chickens, among others. In 2015, the last full year of its operation, the Spirit of the Hills sanctuary took in $156,000 in revenues and incurred $200,000 in expenses for a loss of $44,000. In the previous five years, the sanctuary either lost money or barely broke even. Although the intentions of the director, staff, and volunteers were noble and their efforts noteworthy, the sanctuary was clearly overextended and unable to care for its animals.

Running a wild animal sanctuary is like fusing a zoo with a first-responder rescue operation and managing the whole thing on a not-for-profit's donation-dependent budget. Regardless of how altruistic or soft-hearted a sanctuary owner or director may feel toward the animals in his or her care, running a sanctuary requires making the tough decisions of a for-profit business. An enduring love for animals may motivate someone to start a wildlife sanctuary, but if that love is not tempered and informed by hard-headed business decisions, the animal suffering that the sanctuary is working so hard to alleviate will instead be compounded. It is impossible to save a suffering animal if you then lose the home you wanted to give it in the first place.

From Silver Springs to Golden Dreams

There are large rescues in terms of *number* of animals, and then there are large rescues in terms of pure *tonnage*. The rescue of three adult Kodiak bears – Max, Forest, and Jake – tipping the scales at nearly one ton apiece, is illustrative of the latter.

The colossal and magnificent Kodiak bear, also known as the Alaskan brown bear, is native to the archipelago of Kodiak islands that tail into the Pacific Ocean southwest of Anchorage. One of the two largest bears in the world (the other is the polar bear), it measures five feet at the shoulder with all four feet on the ground and twice that when standing fully upright on its hind legs.

Max, Forest, and Jake, however, were not rescued from Alaska. They were rescued from Silver Springs resort in Florida, which is about as far as you can get from Alaska and still be in the United States. It is far not only in terms of distance – more than 5,000 miles – but in terms of climate. The Kodiak islands are classified as a subpolar oceanic climate, characterized by cold temperatures; persistently cloudy days accompanied by misty, foggy, and windy conditions; and incessant rains. Temperatures rarely climb above 60 degrees. Summers are short and cool; winters are very long, very dark, and very cold. By contrast, Silver Springs is east of Ocala, Florida, a subtropical climate where the summers are very hot, unbearably humid, and intolerably oppressive. Summer temperatures average 90 degrees; the brief and mild winters see average daily temperatures in the lower 70s.

You can see where we are going here. It makes you wonder why anyone ever thought that it was a good idea to put Kodiak bears from Alaska on display in Florida?

Clearly someone did because the bears had been acquired by Silver Springs in the late-1990s as part of management's burgeoning fascination with exotic animal exhibits. The tourist attraction had long been famous for its glass bottom boats, providing views of fish and marine life in the Silver River, as well as its pioneer village, amusement park rides, and other entertainments. The increasing number of exotic and native animals was a more recent and ambitious undertaking. In addition to native species such as tropical birds, alligators, and assorted smaller reptiles, Silver Springs began bringing in bears, mountain lions, giraffes, and other non-native species, ultimately adding up to more than 350 animals.

The World of Bears display was billed as "the largest bear exhibit of its kind in the world," presumably due to the bulk of its four Kodiak inhabitants, supplemented by about ten black bears and spectacled bears. Each of the bears lived in a 400- to 750-square foot caged, concrete exercise yard with an air-conditioned den and miniscule pool. These enclosures were not visible to the public. The Kodiaks were rotated into a 40,000 square foot public display area for two to three hours at a time. The black and spectacled bears were alternated between much smaller 12,000 and 6,000 square foot enclosures. Kodiak bear Max and his brother Lewie, who had grown up together and were both declawed on the front paws, were rotated into and out of the display area together. Similarly, two of the other Kodiak bears, Forest and Jake, also were let in and out of the display together. But the four bears were not displayed together, presumably due to concerns over conflicts in the small area.

7.7 Kodiak bear Max in his concrete exercise yard

Over the roughly fifteen years the Kodiaks were held in captivity in Florida, they lost their heavy, shaggy coats. YouTube videos and photos show almost naked bears lumbering around the enclosure and easing into tiny pools. They became more and more lethargic. They slept most of the day in their dens, an unnatural behavior for these wide-ranging foragers. Without the temperature changes needed to signal seasonal changes, they never hibernated.

Then in December 2006, with Max secured and sleeping in his concrete enclosure, Forest and Jake were accidentally rotated into the display area while Lewie was still there. They attacked Lewie, who they perceived as an intruder, and inflicted fatal injuries – all in front of a throng of tourists and park employees who initially thought the three giants were playing. When Lewie's ear was ripped off, the seriousness of the assault became obvious and tourists were hurried out of the area. The two attackers were finally driven away from their victim with birdshot fired by a deputy from the local county sheriff's office. The fight was said to have lasted about ninety minutes. Lewie died that night from his injuries.

In 2013, with attendance and revenues in rapid decline and the facility becoming more rundown, arrangements were made for Silver Springs to be taken over by the state of Florida. State officials agreed to get rid of the animals and turn the facility into a state park. By May 2013, the resort had closed the animal exhibits and moved most of the animals to other locations. There remained only the three Kodiak bears, five black bears, and three mountain lions. Officials called Pat and he agreed to take the animals. That is when the rescue became "monumental" and, rather unexpectedly, monumentally entertaining.

Silver Springs volunteered to have animal keepers and staff assist with loading the animals in transport cages. So, Pat readied one of the big rigs and set out for Florida alone. It was his first Kodiak rescue. He remembers, "their size was stunning, with heads approaching nearly thirty inches in diameter...and their standing heights of over ten feet...weighing in somewhere around 1,500 to 1,600 pounds. These were amazing creatures both in size and intelligence." Thunderously growling, pounding, and pushing on his enclosure's barred steel door, which "bowed back and forth as if it were made of cardboard or plastic," Max made it abundantly clear that the visitors standing outside his small yard were not welcome. Warned by the animal keeper about riling up the monstrous Kodiaks, the team quickly unloaded a transport cage at Max's door hoping he would become accustomed to it, and then moved on to the easy part of the endeavor, loading up the five black bears and three mountain lions.

When Pat went back to the Kodiaks, it was clear that Max had not adjusted to the uninvited cage. When Pat politely asked Max, Forest, and Jake to walk into their respective transport cages, as their black bear brethren had done, they politely declined. They were not going to enter strange cages under any circumstances. "Nope, nada, not a chance," Pat remembers. The crew was not going to be able to load the Kodiaks without administering a sedative that could be reversed once each of the big bruins was securely in the trailer. Standard Sanctuary operating procedure in such cases is to roll the sleeping bear onto a reinforced nylon gurney with handles that are used to lift the animal through the door of the cage. As a rule of thumb, you could figure on needing about six people to lift an adult grizzly bear.

Max was tranquilized and the team of eight, including one giant of a man who could have been an offensive lineman for the Jacksonville Jaguars, positioned themselves around the bear. Then they braced their legs and set their backs into rolling Max onto the gurney. Max did not budge. At all. "It was hilarious," says Pat, shaking his head.

> Two people could take his whole leg and bend it all the way across his body to the ground and nothing would move, not even an inch. There was just so much mass in the center that it didn't matter. There wasn't enough leverage to move him...No matter what angle, how hard we pushed, or what strategy we employed, his body and head remained in the same spot where he went to sleep...After twenty minutes of insanely strenuous effort, and all eight people nearly passing out from the 97 percent humidity and 98 degree heat...I'm like, oh my God, now what are we going to do? Everybody is grabbing and tugging and pulling and it's hot as hell and we're all just dying, and we haven't moved him an inch yet.

It was time to regroup and figure out plan B, which involved plywood, two by four pieces of lumber, a Waste Management Bagster rated for a 3,300 pound load, and a Telehandler. With the tools at hand, the reinvigorated team levered each bear onto the plywood using the two by fours and then dragged the bear down a narrow passage to a forklift. The forklift tipped the bear onto the Bagster, which was then hoisted over an adjacent sixteen foot tall fence by the Telehandler's crane. To get each bear through the narrow door of the transport cage, the group flipped each cage on its side, removed the door to gain a few inches and lowered each bear down. Pat smiles, "Just like a big blob of Jell-O," each bear "hit the door and gravity took over. Each massive beast slipped through its doorway like a buttered water balloon through grandma's hands at a Fourth of July picnic."

Once at the Sanctuary, the Kodiak bears moved into new multi-acre habitats after a short time in introductory enclosures. As the days grew shorter and the green prairie grasses turned to gold, the big bears began sleeping more. Hibernating over the winter of 2014 – probably for the first

7.8 A bear in a Bagster: Max being lifted over
the fence at Silver Springs

7.9 No, the cage did not shrink: the enormous Kodiaks arrive at the Sanctuary

time in their lives – did wonders for all three. They emerged rested and furry, gaining weight and muscle over the course of the summer.

While at Silver Springs, Max had suffered a debilitating injury. A guillotine gate, a type of heavy gate that can be raised and lowered vertically from a distance using a pulley system, fell and crushed vertebrae in his back. When he arrived at the Sanctuary he was in constant and debilitating pain, his back legs barely able to carry his weight. Yet even he emerged from his den able to walk gingerly around his habitat. As spring and summer progressed, the benefits of a healthy diet and a substantial pool for swimming continued to do the trick and Max's mobility improved. As Pat has remarked, "He knew the value of hydrotherapy, which helped take some of the weight off his enormous frame. Anti-inflammatory drugs along with mild pain medications allowed Max to gently exercise while spending hours a day...in his large custom-made swimming pool." The length of his daily walks around the habitat increased in distance and frequency.

Max lived for six blissful years at the Sanctuary and became a favorite of visitors. He was famous for both his indomitable spirit and his mighty snores, which vibrated across the land in all directions during his frequent afternoon naps in the summer sun. Pat remembers, "Max was truly a giant teddy bear with a gentle soul that deserved so much more than what life gave him. He should never have had to live in an amusement park or become injured so severely. He should have been born in the wilds of Kodiak Island and been able to live among other giants that thrive in that unique environment...We were blessed to have known him."

7.10 Max

Chapter 8

🐾🐾🐾🐾🐾🐾🐾🐾🐾🐾🐾🐾🐾🐾🐾🐾
🐾🐾🐾🐾🐾🐾🐾🐾🐾🐾🐾🐾🐾🐾🐾🐾

Around the World and Back Again:
The Trials of International Rescues

"Lambert," the orange-clad volunteer remarks casually as we gaze down at a smallish and impossibly thin male lion ensconced in one of the enclosures in the Lion House, "was just rescued from Saipan along with a tiger named Tasha Joy." Saipan? We glance at each other. We had never heard of Saipan. Where on earth is Saipan? The volunteer moves away to answer another visitor's questions and we immediately pull out an iPhone to search for Saipan on the map app. A tiny island appears north of Guam; it is a speck of sand in the vastness of the Pacific Ocean. There is a storybook quality to the tale: Once upon a time on a tiny link in a chain of islands called the Marianas, there lived a lion named Lambert and a tiger named Tasha Joy. They were rescued by defenders of captive wildlife who transported them halfway around the world to a magical new home at the Sanctuary. Now Lambert is twenty feet below us and Tasha Joy a ten minute walk away.

Lambert is our introduction to the Sanctuary's international rescues. We are amazed that the team would go to such great lengths to rescue a single lion and a single tiger from so far away. Little did we know at the time that more than 100 of the roughly 500 animals currently living at the Sanctuary had been rescued from outside the United States.

When visitors first learn of the many international rescues by The Wild Animal Sanctuary over the decades, they are as surprised as we were. But once you get to know the Sanctuary, the daring rescues of animals from all over the world seem quite natural. Remarkable, yes. Unexpected, no. In fact, they embody the very spirit of the organization. Three lionesses from Panama in 2011? No problem! A dozen African lions and four bears from Spain in 2015? Of course! Three tigers from a failing zoo in Argentina? We are there! Indeed, at some point, the idea of *not rescuing* animals just because they are halfway around the world seems like the more shocking and unfathomable choice.

The international rescue work of the Sanctuary clearly demonstrates that the captive wildlife problem extends well beyond America's borders. Individuals who want to own an exotic pet and exploiters of wild animals for entertainment or medicinal purposes can be found across the planet. Pat Craig has observed, "Up until about fifteen years ago it was purely an American problem. Then it started to become an international problem."

Over almost three decades, the Sanctuary has rescued close to 200 animals in ten countries on four continents. Of course, the numbers are constantly changing as new calls come in asking for help from a burgeoning network of those committed to captive wildlife rescue around the world.

Pat is one of the few captive wildlife advocates who knows his way around the legal, regulatory, permitting, and import/export red tape that often confounds even those sanctuaries with the best of international rescue intentions. Federal and state laws dealing with the import and transport of exotic wildlife are complex. There are highly detailed regulations that must be followed without deviation to protect the safety and welfare of the animal being imported, safeguard the health and welfare of the American public, and ensure that the laws of the affected countries are respected.

An exotic animal import document can easily run to 100 pages, and even more if the animal is on the Endangered Species List. Forms are long and detailed; "i's" must be dotted and "t's" must be crossed. Health certificates are mandatory. Signatures are essential. Timing is critical. And it is not just the paperwork. Cages or crates must provide suitable ventilation, space, and protection. Their contents, as well as origination and destination points, must be clearly labeled. Myriad government regulations and airline rules deal with the flight itself, including the range of acceptable outdoor temperatures (if it is too hot or too cold outside the animal is not permitted to fly), food and water requirements, sedation prohibitions (animals should not be sedated for a flight), and health checks upon arrival. Inspections are conducted by U.S. Customs and Border Protection (CBP). Everything must be done by the book lest the USDA, USFWS, Centers for Disease Control (CDC), or some other government agency throw the book at you. And that just touches upon import regulations on the U.S. side; export regulations from the foreign country can be equally, if not more, daunting.

Because of his decades of experience with complex transnational operations, Pat is often the first person called when an animal is in need in a foreign country or when an international rescue operation already underway runs into a morass of paperwork and logistical problems. It is not a job for amateurs. Over the years, he has learned where the rocky shoals of exotic animal importation are and how to navigate around them. Just as every rescue in the United States is unique, so is every international rescue.

When Fortunes Change: The Rescue of Leonardo

Wild animal rescues, whether domestic or international, always begin with a call for help. Most typically by phone, or more recently via text message and email, someone reaches out to Pat at the Sanctuary. Sometimes the call comes in from an overseas organization that Pat has worked with on more than one rescue; other times it's a voice he has never heard before; often it's someone immersed in the select yet ever expanding network of wild animal advocates that stretches across the globe. Over the years, hundreds of international calls have come in, but as with anything, it is often the "firsts" that stay with us.

For Pat, the first international rescue call came in 1994. With fewer than fifty animals, the Sanctuary was less than a tenth of the size it is today. "There is," the official explained, "an African lion in a cage outside a fortune teller's shop in Puebla, a town south of Mexico City. His name is Leonardo, Léon for short. He isn't doing well."

Leonardo, who at the time of his rescue was probably about six years old, lived in a tiny barred cage on a street in a little town south of the Mexican capital. The fortune teller had used the lion as a ploy to stop pedestrians in mid-stride so he could lure them into his shop. Now the fortune teller was struggling to make ends meet and could not afford to feed the lion. So, he wanted to get rid of it. The caller arranged to meet Pat at the shop to translate and help with the exchange.

Pat agreed to drive the more than 1,700 miles to Puebla, admitting, "I couldn't fathom flying an animal at this point. So, I got in the truck and drove down to the center of Mexico, which was an insane journey in and of itself. It was Mad Max Beyond Thunderdome sort of stuff. And then I got to the little town and it was just me and the person who initiated the thing. She spoke Spanish. I didn't speak a lick of Spanish, so she was talking to the fortune teller guy." She translated for Pat the sorrow of Leonardo's life. The fortune teller had put him in the cage as a cub and had never taken him out of the cage, so it was rusted shut. Leonardo was skinny, but he was a big boy, and he was a mess. His long, heavy mane was hopelessly matted, and he was covered in feces and urine. Pat had to sedate the lion in order to break through the rusty bars, then get him out of the cage and loaded into a clean cage on the truck – and then drive the thirty-plus hours back to the Sanctuary.

Pat had already researched the permits he needed to get Leonardo through customs at the U.S.-Mexico border. "Nowadays, he relates, "we get all the permits before we even leave Keenesburg. In those days, you had to still do the permits, but you could do them at the border. You had to deal with the Mexican side to get them to stamp the export permit. Then you would go to the American side and do the import process." It all seemed relatively straightforward. But when Pat got to the border, things went downhill in a hurry. He found himself on a ten-lane, one-way superhighway in a sea of traffic sprinting northbound to the U.S. customs checkpoint. He could see the Mexican side where he needed to have the export permits stamped; it had its own ten-lane, one-way southbound superhighway. But there was no road between them and no way to get there. Although only about a half mile away, it may as well have been ten miles. He was trapped between vehicles on all sides, but even if he had been the only car on the road, short of hammering the truck into four-wheel drive and taking the overland route, which might have resulted in a lively police chase, there was no way to cross over to Mexican customs. He remembers vividly his alarm at "being sucked up to the U.S.-Mexico border."

> I'm going crazy trying to figure it out. I've got a lion in here! I've got to get him across the border! How do I get over there to do this permit? I'm sweating it. There's no way. I'm stuck in traffic moving toward the U.S. border and I keep looking for any way out. Finally I get up to the U.S. border and I'm freaking out, thinking everyone is going to be really pissed I haven't finished the permits.

He took a deep breath and hastened to explain to the American guard that he hadn't been able to have the export paperwork authorized, "I've got this lion and I've got to get over to Mexico and get the export permit stamped and cancelled." The American customs agent looked at him quizzically, then remarked, "What the hell do you care? You're on American soil! You're here!"

So much for the Mexican export permit; Pat and Leonardo were in the U.S. The customs agent stamped the import permit. Then he asked to see Leonardo, unwittingly kicking off a scenario that would play out again and again in international rescues where inspections and checkpoints are commonplace. Regardless of whether the Sanctuary team is crossing a border, loading transport cages into a cargo bay, or departing from or landing at an international airport, people want to see the wild animals the Sanctuary team has in tow. After all, it is not every day that African lions, grizzlies, Asiatic black bears, jaguars, or tigers break the tedium of an otherwise humdrum workaday shift. Curiosity about the Sanctuary's cargo has resulted in both private showings and pressing throngs of onlookers. Pat smiles, "there's always a giant crowd at border security or people who handle the cargo…you just let them come up with cell phones and do their pictures and then go on and do your thing. It's always crazy." And it has happened with almost every international rescue. The only difference is that, unlike the customs agent who gave Leonardo a big assist in his move to the United States almost three decades ago and just wanted to take a peek at him, today everyone wants to take a selfie with which to regale family and friends.

In any case, that is how Leonardo came to the U.S and how international rescues came to the Sanctuary. "That's all it took," Pat recalls, "just that one rescue." Leonardo's rescue led to another and another south of the border. Pat continued to offer the Sanctuary's help if the local initiators did the groundwork by getting owners to voluntarily surrender their big cats or other animals to the Sanctuary and in taking care of logistics. "I would always just think, man, if people knew how many people had been involved to save this one animal's life, they would be blown away. I was blown away…It took everybody doing what they did to make it happen. These weren't even organizations; these were just people." They were just people doing their best to move the ball forward on alleviating animal suffering. Over the years their valiant efforts continued to build.

Lions and Bears from Barcelona: The Murphy's Law of Animal Rescues

Lions and grizzly bears were in dire straits in Barcelona. Once part of Aqualeón, a drive-through animal park where wildlife roamed in large acreage habitats, the animals had become the responsibility of the Spanish government when the financially failing park shut down. With government officials equally stymied in their efforts to achieve fiscal solvency for the animal park, the free-roaming animals were captured and placed inside tiny concrete pens. Some animals were rehomed. Nine long years passed. Only one lion pride and four bears remained out of the original twenty-eight animals captured. Finally, in 2014, Spanish officials contacted the Sanctuary. That is when the international paperwork and logistics problems started.

Months passed, delays ensued, and costs skyrocketed as local veterinarians and officials with no experience in international animal transport grappled with the hundreds of details inherent in moving large carnivores. For starters, the original air transport plan was unworkable. The lions and bears were scheduled on a cargo flight from Barcelona to Chicago, with a layover in Luxembourg. The flight from Luxembourg, however, was scheduled to land at O'Hare on a Sunday, a clear violation of that airport's animal transport policy, which prohibited such arrivals on weekends. So, the Chicago flight was rescheduled for Monday. Problem solved? Not really, because the original Barcelona to Luxembourg flight was not changed to accommodate the new transatlantic flight schedule. The plane would simply arrive in Luxembourg on Saturday and park until its allotted flight time to Chicago on Monday. The animals would have to remain in their small cages in the cargo hold for at least twenty-four hours – without care, food, and possibly fresh water. With the situation becoming increasingly untenable, the Sanctuary refused to accept the wild animals unless a new flight plan was put into place.

Although the cost nearly doubled, the animals were finally booked on a direct, non-stop flight from Barcelona to O'Hare, scheduled to arrive on a Monday. The Sanctuary team was there to meet the animals, finish up the paperwork, oversee the health checks, and then drive them in the Sanctuary's special transport trailers to Colorado. It seemed that soon everyone could breathe a sigh of relief. But, unfortunately, the setbacks were hardly over.

When the animals arrived in Chicago, it was clear that the Spanish veterinarian had sedated the animals, in clear violation of animal welfare laws. The animals also were bedded down in straw, another violation of USDA regulations prohibiting the import of raw agricultural products due to the diseases that might be introduced here and the insects that might be buried within. Sure enough, an "army of bugs just so happened to hitch a ride by stowing away within the suspect straw." As if those were not problems enough, raw meat had been tossed in the cages, which was yet another violation of U.S. protocol governing the importation of raw meat. And there sat the sixteen blameless animals, victims of what had become a perfect storm of biohazard and animal welfare violations.

The Sanctuary rescue team offloaded the cages and secured them inside an international shipping terminal. Then they got to work with the USDA, USFWS, and CBP. The authorities decided the animals (along with the straw and the bugs and the raw meat) had to go into quarantine. But where? There was no place to keep sixteen large carnivores at O'Hare or anywhere else nearby. The USDA and other agencies finally agreed that the Sanctuary's sealed and climate controlled transport trailers could serve as mobile quarantine facilities to transport the animals back to Colorado. Once there, the Sanctuary vehicles, crates, and their occupants would be secured inside a quarantine building and the cleanup and decontamination process could commence. The rescue team wearily reloaded the animals and began the long drive back to Colorado.

USDA and other government officials met the Sanctuary rescue team in Colorado to observe and monitor the quarantine and cleanup operation needed to ensure that neither the animals nor the environment were harmed. Over the course of five busy days, the cages were emptied, and the animals released into their new homes. A company specializing in biohazard waste disposal and toxic cleanups scoured the crates, the trailers, and the quarantine site and then bagged the potentially hazardous organic material (one would have to think this was one of the crew's more unique assignments) and hauled it away for incineration.

Animal care staff began administering arthritis medication to the four bears, each at least thirty years old. With enormous habitats in which they could now shuffle around in classic bear fashion, the best food available, and personal attention to their care and overall well-being, Changao, Pipo, Jacky, and Rubia began to thrive.

8.1 Rubia enjoying a dip in the pool

8.2 The Spain lions beneath a rainbow shade structure

The lions: Rubio Joven, Melena Negra, Bruno, Bartolo, Diablo, and lionesses: Lara, Flora, Nala, Patricia, Miedica also settled in quickly, roaming about enormous habitats which may have been somewhat reminiscent of the wildlife park outside Barcelona. Each lion and lion pride at the Sanctuary has a certain personality. We might characterize the "Spain" lions as a wild bunch – fiercely protective of their territories and, for the most part, aloof with their caregivers. Given the size of the safari park in which they roamed prior to their nine-year incarceration in small cages, the pride members may have had little or virtually no contact with humans. Alternatively, they may carry scars from having had too much contact with callous and cruel people. As with so many of the animals rescued by the Sanctuary, we will never know what they really went through before they came here; we simply accept them on their own terms.

Good Samaritans are Alive and Well: The Rescue of Lambert and Tasha Joy

Bill Nimmo and Kizmin Reeves called in late 2018. Big – and small – cat lovers, the husband and wife team had started Tigers in America (TIA) after organizing the rescue of seven tigers from a failing sanctuary in Texas. What they thought would be an isolated gesture of goodwill instead opened the floodgates of the captive wildlife crisis across the United States. Once word of their generosity got out, the calls started coming in from Ohio, Mississippi, Missouri, Arkansas, Wisconsin. With the extent of the captive tiger problem becoming clearer and clearer, they found themselves with a renewed passion and a new vocation for saving tigers from the horrors of abuse and neglect. Since establishing TIA they have been involved with the rescue and relocation of more than 280 tigers as well as other big cats, bears, and smaller wild carnivores.

The rescue that Bill contacted Pat about in November 2018 was much farther afield. TIA had gotten a call from APHIS about an African lion and a tiger at a failed zoo on the island of Saipan. The island had just been decimated by a super typhoon. The APHIS official had asked TIA if they knew of a sanctuary that could send people to Saipan, fly the lion and tiger back to the U.S., and provide them a home. TIA immediately recommended The Wild Animal Sanctuary, and so began a whirlwind rescue mission in the wake of the typhoon.

Logistics for the rescue over the next few weeks both on the ground in Keenesburg and then on the island of Saipan involved TIA, the Federal Emergency Management Agency (FEMA) and the USDA, as well as FEDEX and Samaritan's Purse, a not-for-profit charitable organization that brings humanitarian aid to those in need. Not only did Samaritan's Purse bring in disaster relief for the people on the island, it also provided the cargo transport that airlifted the two big cats off the island. In this case the name was prophetic because this rescue halfway around the world was made possible only because of the help of Good Samaritans every step of the way.

At just twelve miles long and less than six miles wide, Saipan is part of the Northern Mariana Islands, an archipelago of more than a dozen islands lying about 120 miles north of Guam. Saipan has been a U.S. commonwealth since 1978; people born there are U.S. citizens and the currency is the U.S. dollar. Fewer than 60,000 people live in the Northern Mariana Islands and ninety percent of them live on Saipan. Think of Hawaii – turquoise and topaz blue waters, fluffy clouds gathering on endless ocean horizons, white sand beaches, and swaying palm trees. The weather is lovely in this tropical paradise unless, of course, a typhoon is bearing down on the island. Typhoons are a way of life in this part of the world and they can be nasty. For locals, the basic barometer of storm severity is whether the banana trees have survived the onslaught.

Super typhoons occur less frequently but when these monster storms slam into tiny Pacific islands, total wreckage follows in their wake. A super typhoon is defined as a storm that reaches maximum sustained winds of 150 miles per hour – roughly equivalent to a Cat 5 hurricane in the United States. In October 2018, Super Typhoon Yutu, which tied for the strongest storm anywhere in the world that year, devastated Saipan and the Northern Mariana Islands. Two hundred mile an hour winds leveled buildings. Massive flooding and sporadic fires took out many of the remaining structures. Power, clean water, and basic services were ravaged. Great portions of the island were reduced to rubble. The banana trees did not survive.

As always, when a typhoon or hurricane moves on to ravage its next victims, relief services and humanitarian aid organizations flood in. Various government agencies and all manner of charitable organizations begin the process of flying in staff and supplies and doling out food, water, blankets, and medicines; restoring power and water utilities; getting people into temporary housing; clearing out debris; and settling in for the long and wearisome task of rebuilding the infrastructure. Calls also come in for animal relief aid.

When Bill and Kizmin called, Pat knew exactly what sort of challenges lie ahead. Having carried out dozens of international rescues he knew firsthand the complexity of the task he would be facing. The situation in Saipan was grim. With Herculean humanitarian efforts underway to aid the people of Saipan, it was unlikely that anyone would be able to focus on two big cats in a neglected and forgotten zoo. The tiger and lion were without food, water, or shelter and would likely die in a few weeks. Pat knew it would be nearly impossible to bring in proper food, specially built air cargo cages, transport vehicles, and veterinary supplies; process the necessary paperwork; and safely get the two animals off the island quickly. Running the gauntlet of a large carnivore rescue operation while disaster relief cargo planes were streaming in with personnel and supplies to care for the desperate residents of the island had hopelessness written all over it.

When Pat received photos of the tiger and lion that had been taken *before* the storm hit, he was horrified. The cats were clearly starving to death. The fifteen-year old African lion was skeletal. His ribs, hip bones and vertebrae protruded through his skin. A fully grown lion should weigh 400 pounds or more; the lion in the photo probably weighed less than half that. The tiger was equally emaciated, with thin limbs, and little visible muscle. The stripes along her flanks were punctuated by every rib. It was obvious to Pat that the two animals would be lucky to last a few days, let alone a few weeks. Their rescue should have been coordinated months if not years before. If the Sanctuary was not able to act quickly, it might not be able to act at all.

8.3 Lambert in Saipan 8.4 Tasha Joy in Saipan

Yet, by some stroke of luck, serendipity, providence or all three, every time the situation seemed impossible, the pieces would unexpectedly fall into place and a Good Samaritan – or two or three – would enter the picture. Good Samaritan number one, a FEMA official on the island, had discovered the animals. After seeing the dreadful state of the two big cats, she asked the acting military commander responsible for managing air traffic in and out of the islands if the large carnivores could somehow be ferried out on an empty cargo plane bound for the United States. While skeptical, he agreed to investigate possibilities. The next day the commander found himself talking to two airline cargo pilots who were about to fly an empty plane back to the U.S. to pick up another load of disaster supplies. When the commander asked them about the possibility of flying the two big cats back to the U.S. on a later flight, they agreed to run the idea by management. That makes for Good Samaritans two, three and four.

In fact, the pilots worked for Samaritan's Purse (which would turn out to be Good Samaritan number five). Inspired by the story of the Good Samaritan in the Gospel of Luke, Samaritan's Purse is a North Carolina-based, nondenominational Christian organization run by Reverend Franklin Graham. It provides aid around the world to those who are poor, sick, and suffering. Samaritan's Purse not only agreed to fly the animals out, it also offered to fly the Sanctuary team to Saipan to collect the animals. Everything was coming together. But new challenges kept popping up.

The latest trial was the timing of the flight to Saipan, which was scheduled to leave Piedmont Triad International Airport outside of Greensboro in just four days! There was no way the Sanctuary team could get everything ready and drive the international shipping crates and other equipment and supplies from Colorado to North Carolina in just a few days. Enter Good Samaritan number six, this time under the guise of FEDEX, who agreed to pick up the crates, equipment, and supplies at the Sanctuary and fly them to Greensboro. At that point, with a logistical target in sight, the Sanctuary's rescue team flew into high gear. Becca took charge of the medical side; Casey focused on readying two break-down aluminum shipping crates; and Ryan ensured that labels, equipment, materials, and meds were inside the crates so the whole shebang could be shrink-wrapped for shipping. Pat and Casey got ready to catch an eastbound flight to Greensboro, where they would meet Bill Nimmo and catch the Samaritan's Purse DC-8 cargo plane westbound for Saipan.

TIA also had been working Saipan logistics. The first order of business was to find a truck with a crane able to lift the transport cages onto the truck bed. Good Samaritan number seven stepped up when members of the USDA emergency relief team found what may have been the only such truck available on the island. TIA also dispatched funds to USDA officials in Saipan so the big cats could be given fresh meat on a daily basis and to enlist the services of a local veterinarian who could sign off on the health certificates needed to get them out of Saipan. Fortunately, because Saipan is part of the United States, the international paperwork trail was minimized. More Good Samaritans in the way of U.S. federal agency personnel and the local veterinarian came to check on the cats.

Given the heavy load of disaster relief supplies and the substantial fuel consumption of the loaded cargo plane, it was going to be a long journey from North Carolina to Saipan. With a brief stop for refueling in Phoenix, an overnight stop in Hawaii so the pilots could comply with FAA pilot fatigue regulations, and the loss of a day after crossing the International Dateline, it took three days for the Sanctuary team to get to Saipan.

Incredibly, when the cargo plane touched down, the truck with the crane was waiting at the airport. Although the lion, now known as Lambert, and the tiger, now known as Tasha Joy, did not know it, they were about to begin a journey that would change their lives. With barely enough daylight left to get a quick look at the two animals, the team hurried to the zoo to talk to the owner and begin assembling the transport crates. There they learned that the zoo had long been suffering from financial woes. The owner was unable to provide for the animals, and in fact a black bear and a leopard had already died from neglect. Unfortunately and shamefully, the owner never took the actions he could have to secure a better home for the animals in his care. Sadly, it took Super Typhoon Yutu to get help for the suffering animals.

With the diet of nutritious fresh meat courtesy of TIA, Lambert and Tasha Joy had even perked up a bit. Sequestered on opposite ends of the small zoo, the two animals did not know each other at all. Even more alarming was that Lambert did not know he was a lion and Tasha Joy seemed clueless about the fact that she was a tiger. Both African lions and tigers are highly vocal and garrulous animals. Lions are justifiably famous for their enormous roars, but they also emit moans, whimpers, meows, grunts, snarls, hums, and other audible signals of lion jargon and chitchat to communicate with each other. Tigers chuff, moan, groan, and use all manner of verbal signals to tell you how they're doing, what their day has been like, whether they are in a good mood or bad, and how glad they are to see you. But Lambert and Tasha Joy said nothing. They were completely and eerily silent. Having been purchased as cubs from a Guam zoo fifteen years before, both had lived in solitary confinement in the intervening years and simply did not know how to talk. Pat describes the first moments:

> The one thing that stood out the most with both cats was their lack of social graces. Neither Lambert nor Tasha knew their own language or how to communicate in general since each had lived solitarily the entire time they were there. Although Lambert seemed glad to see us, he never made a sound while we spoke to him, even when he rolled over or came toward us in a playful manner…Tasha was no different, gazing at us with a completely blank expression as we chuffed and lovingly moaned sweet aphorisms her way.

The Sanctuary team worked to develop a trusting relationship with the big cats, talking, gesturing to, and working quietly with them over the next couple of days. Tasha Joy began emitting "tiny truncated chuffs as she would pass by during repeated laps around the interior of her cage." Finally, she had enough confidence to gaze into the eyes of her new caregivers, evidence that she had been aching for attention and affection. Tasha Joy "slowly began to chuff louder and more freely as her confidence in us grew." Lambert too kept trying to communicate and, amazingly, Pat remembers, "It wasn't long before Lambert began to mimic our low guttural moans and deep puffing sounds, which are all positive solicitations in lion tongue. He also began feeble attempts at roaring to call us back each time we would leave to go check on Tasha. It was very uplifting to see how hard he was trying to open lines of communication with us."

8.5 Pat and Tasha Joy in Saipan

When it was time to go to the airport, both big cats settled down in their new crates ready to begin the journey to their new home on the other side of the world. With the now-empty cargo bay, save a lion and a tiger and a Sanctuary team, the flight was a direct, nonstop fourteen hours to Denver International Airport (DIA). The last Good Samaritan of the operation – and we have lost count of how many there were – was Signature Air, the flight base operation at DIA, who offered their terminal and offloading equipment to get Lambert and Tasha Joy safely off the plane and into an enclosed Sanctuary rescue vehicle.

Upon arriving at the Sanctuary, both big cats spent a couple of days in the Clinic under observation. Having lived without other tigers for all those years, Tasha Joy saw no reason to start up any new relationships at this point. Her snarls and aloof behavior at the Tiger Roundhouse signaled in no uncertain terms that she was looking for a single room, so to speak. Respecting her wishes, the Sanctuary moved Tasha Joy to a substantial enclosure across from the Roundhouse. Large, lush, and shaded, with platforms for climbing and a lovely den for getting away from it all, her new home was only about fifteen feet away from tigers Athos and Frida, so tiger chuffs and smells became part and parcel of Tasha Joy's new world.

Once at the Sanctuary Lambert was quickly moved to the Lion House, recuperative facility extraordinaire for African lions from all over the world. The Lion House is justifiably famous for its role in facilitating the Bolivian Lion Rescue described in the next chapter and its fame in establishing the Sanctuary as a go-to place for large carnivores.

But for us, the Lion House is also where Lambert learned to roar.

8.6 Tasha Joy at the Sanctuary

8.7 Lambert relaxing in the Lion House

When you are inside the Lion House on the observation deck, the space reverberates with African lion roars coming from residents inside the ClearSpan structure and those outside in larger habitats. The Lion House is an echo chamber, a symphony of lion music. The roars build to a crescendo and then begin to fade without warning into a series of low pitched grunts. For a little lion who lacked the stature of his mightier and more well-nourished brethren, Lambert's formidable roars filled the Lion House. There he finally learned that he is a lion, king of the beasts, member of a great chorus, carrying on the way lions have for thousands of years.

For close to a year Lambert steadily gained weight in the comfort of the Lion House and under the care of the Sanctuary team. But he did not seem to be thriving in quite the way that everyone had hoped. Concerned about parasites or worse, Lambert was transported in the Sanctuary ambulance to Colorado State University. Exploratory surgery found inoperable cancer. Sadly, a few months later, Tasha Joy also died from cancer.

"It happens," Pat laments, "the Sanctuary takes in rescued animals, many of whom are older and have been malnourished and suffering for most of their lives and you are watching them improve and then all of a sudden it just takes a turn and you get blindsided by something you weren't expecting...That's part of the reality people need to know."

So many Sanctuary rescues arrive beaten down by life and by people who cared not one whit about them. Some last only a few weeks. Others live at the Sanctuary for decades. Some who are not expected to live more than a few days end up enjoying years under the loving care of Pat and the Sanctuary team. As volunteers, we thrill at the arrival of every animal who comes to the Sanctuary. We revel in their recoveries from abuse. We bless the freedoms they enjoy in their new home. We mourn their passing.

Dr. Felicia Knightly has remarked, "These animals are amazingly stoic... to see the way they respond to kindness is amazing. Even if they do not get here until they are nineteen and they live only one more year, or even two months. That's two months of the best life they have ever had." The Wild Animal Sanctuary *is* the best life they have ever had.

In truth, for the many of the rescues who have endured what most of us could not bear, even *one day* at the Sanctuary is a gift beyond measure. Lambert had 405 days at the Sanctuary and Tasha Joy had 517.

Chapter 9

:·: :·: :·: :·: :·: :·: :·: :·: :·: :·: :·: :·: :·: :·: :·: :·:
:·: :·: :·: :·: :·: :·: :·: :·: :·: :·: :·: :·: :·: :·: :·: :·:

Bolivian Lions Come to Colorado

For sheer scale and indomitable will, the operation to save twenty-five African lions from Bolivia in 2011 with Animal Defenders International (ADI) on the deployment side and The Wild Animal Sanctuary on the receiving end was a captive wildlife rescue for the books. It helped put the Sanctuary on the international media map as a player among elite animal rights, legal defense, and rescue operations around the world. It also tested the initiative, resourcefulness, and resolve of the entire Sanctuary team. Indeed, if anything demonstrates clearly the "bias for action" that we have witnessed time and time again and which is part and parcel of the Sanctuary's "can-do" culture, it is the Bolivian lion rescue in which the operations team had to scramble to build a brand new Lion House in six weeks in the dead of winter.

The film *Lion Ark*, produced by ADI, documents the rescue and is memorable for its vivid images of the high-pressure operations on the ground in Bolivia. An incensed 500-pound African lion lunges roaring furiously at the creaking metal bars of its flimsy cage. Another lies so still he might be dead or dying, completely oblivious to the two dozen flies crawling in open sores around his eyes and on his face. Angry circus owners wield weapons and demand reparations. Aging, rickety trucks lurch precariously along mud slicked and deeply rutted dirt roads. These are the *Lion Ark* images that have stayed with us. Dark nights. Torrential rains. High risk confiscations. Suffering. Squalor. Misery. Despair.

But when we think of the twenty-five Bolivian lions airlifted to the Sanctuary in early 2011, what comes to our minds are the magnificent and confident animals that began to emerge just a few weeks and months after settling in at The Wild Animal Sanctuary. Today, we see from the Walkway contented lions relaxing in sumptuous, grassy meadows; loping toward the fences at mealtime; chasing one another through the snow; and roaring gloriously through all the days of a Colorado year. Each one of the twenty-five could have been a poster child for what is possible with enough care, love, patience, and time to heal.

The Bolivian lion rescue was organized by ADI in cooperation with the Bolivian government. Founded in 1990 in the U.K. and managed by Jan Creamer and Tim Phillips, ADI educates the public about animal abuses and suffering, campaigns for legislative changes to end animal abuse, and rescues animals around the world. The mission initiated in the fall of 2010 was to rescue twenty-five lions from eight different Bolivian circuses and find them a new home. In 2009 the Bolivian government had passed Law 4040, which effectively banned the use of all animals in circuses. Animal activists commended Bolivia as the first country to enact and enforce a national ban on animal entertainment. The circus owners, unhappy about seeing their meager livelihood vanish with the stroke of a pen in La Paz, did not see it that way. Law 4040 gave circus owners a year to find new homes for their now-illegal exotic animals. But, in fact, few did so.

When the ADI teams began confiscating the circus lions, they faced infuriated and defiant owners living in horrifically impoverished regions, often controlled by drug cartels. Rescuing the lions at the height of the rainy season meant harrowing and arduous drives over almost impassable roads. Threatened, and threatening, workers slashed tires and tried to disable the rescue vehicles in any way they could. One owner approached the arriving team wielding a knife. Clashes occurred between animal rights activists and circus supporters. Yet even these frightening confrontations among humans were nothing as dreadful as the conditions in which ADI found the animals.

At one circus, the team found eight lions imprisoned in a six foot by twelve foot cage—a space about the size of a two-horse trailer. They formed an agitated and writhing mass of pacing, circling bodies, surging around each other in a pulsating dance of desperation. They slept piled atop one another prostrate in their own urine and squashed feces, skin stretched taught across sharply protruding hip bones, every rib outlined in a testament to their starvation. Dubbed the "Cavalini Eight" after the circus where they were found, these lions endured the most appalling conditions, living their lives out in what can aptly be termed a "beast wagon."

At one point in *Lion Ark*, Colo Colo, a twelve-year old giant male lunges and claws at the bars of a rickety cage in danger of collapse, his snarling, massive teeth only a few inches from Tim Phillips. Phillips later described the scene, "He was full-on aggressive and would lunge at us whenever we got close to the cage. He was trying to kill us. We were a rusty old door away from being attacked."

All total, ADI rescued fourteen males and eleven females. The oldest was a fifteen-year old male named Kimba and the youngest were three, two-month old cubs, who were yet to be named, and their mother Kiara. Most of the lions were dehydrated and suffering from a variety of health problems. Once at the holding area in Santa Cruz, they received the water and food desperately needed by their battered bodies, as well as preliminary medical treatments. Most had infections from living in their own filth. Many suffered from excruciatingly painful dental problems, the extent of which would only later be fully confirmed by Sanctuary staff and veterinary dentists. Kiara's three cubs were treated for parasites. The lions were given straw to lay on and balls to play with – most likely the first soft bedding and recreational enrichment they had ever experienced. Although they still had to bide their time in small cages in Santa Cruz, the lions had begun the journey toward their new home – but the location of that new home had been a challenge all along the way.

In truth, the rescue operation was two-pronged. The first step was confiscating the lions and figuring out how to get them out of Bolivia. The second step was finding them a home somewhere else. The ADI team worked both problems simultaneously. There were few facilities anywhere in the world equipped to handle an influx of that many big cats that quickly, all of whom would need ongoing rehabilitation, medical care, high quality diets, and lion-sized habitats. Finally, in mid-December, Jan Creamer contacted Pat Craig. When Pat immediately agreed to take all the lions, Jan's relief was profound, "This is the dream, a place where these animals who have suffered so much can be free and safe." She continued, "Tim and I have been searching for a home where our family prides can stay together forever. In terms of both cost and animal welfare, it needs to be every lion on one flight to the same destination. And finally we found our dream home nearly 5,000 miles away in Colorado...The Wild Animal Sanctuary."

When he agreed to make a home for twenty-five African lions, Pat had no place in which to house them. But those sorts of hurdles had never stopped him before. He was always working the problem of what was best for his animals. What have they been through? What are they used to? How have they suffered? What medical attention will they need? How will they acclimate to their new conditions? What type of housing and habitats do we need to create for them? And in the case of the Bolivian lions, how quickly can we get this done? The largest lion rescue in history was in the final planning stages 5,000 miles to the south and the Sanctuary needed to be ready when the lions arrived.

As both Jan and Pat knew, the lions would have to be flown to Colorado. Driving them 5,000 miles from Santa Cruz to Denver was out of the question. Local teams began building twenty-two secure airline cargo crates for the journey north. Each of the lions would travel in a separate crate except lioness Kiara and her three cubs.

For the Sanctuary, the winter arrival in Colorado meant lions who had lived their entire lives in moist tropical Bolivia would find themselves coping with freezing nighttime temperatures and quite probably snow. As Kent Drotar put it, the lions would be "arriving with their 'windbreakers' on, not their winter coats." Having cared for big cats for over thirty years and with several dozen lions already in place at the Sanctuary, Pat knew the health-compromised Bolivian lions would struggle to survive their first winter outside. They needed a transitional enclosed space to acclimate to Colorado's much colder and wintry climate. The only answer was to build them a "Lion House." Thinking of the physical and mental anguish that had long been endured by his imminent charges, Pat was hardly content to build anything even closely resembling the dark and dingy warehouses he had seen on too many occasions. "We knew," he explained, "the only option was to build a structure that would be similar to a biosphere, where the lions could live amongst trees, grass and natural sunlight."

The Sanctuary team hit upon the idea of a 15,000 square foot, 150-foot long and 43-foot high ClearSpan structure. It would be cut through longitudinally by a truck-sized tunnel. Eight 1,400-square foot, steel-fenced animal enclosures would be built along the sides of the tunnel, four on the east side and four on the west side, which would provide animal care givers easy access to their charges at ground level. Gates in the fences along the outer walls would provide the lions access to sizable outdoor pens that offered the first step in their adjustment to Colorado's big skies and expansive prairies. A large wooden observation deck would be built on top of the tunnel, enabling staff and later visitors to see the lions below. The trusses and tent covering of the ClearSpan structure would soar over the tunnel, observation deck, and lion enclosures, and be anchored to the ground on either side. The design concept was brilliant and ambitious.

Flying the lions to Denver meant that they would arrive toward the end of January – just six weeks hence. That set an almost impossible timeframe in which to get the Lion House built, particularly given that the Christmas holidays were only days away. As Pat has said, "we had gone from knowing nothing about the Bolivian lions in mid-December to agreeing to provide a permanent 80-acre home with a massive 15,000 square foot biosphere that had to be ready by the end of January."

With no time to spare, the Sanctuary team had at it, working with ClearSpan, procuring materials, contacting subcontractors, and coordinating logistics. Staff and volunteers built the tunnel out of telephone poles, covered it with the 2,000 square foot observation deck, and fenced in eight lion enclosures over the Christmas and New Year's holidays.

When the ClearSpan structural components arrived on January 22, the building was put up in seven days. The Lion House was ready and waiting for its new leonine residents.

When the lions were delayed out of Bolivia by a couple of weeks, the Sanctuary team found some breathing room. Finally on February 16, Operation Lion Ark was ready to end in Santa Cruz. The lions were coaxed into the twenty-two cargo crates, which were loaded up and strapped in place on a giant DC-10 Transportes Aéreos Bolivianos (TAB) air cargo jet. Jan Creamer, Tim Phillips, and ADI veterinarian Mel Richardson buckled up and the plane lifted skyward heading north. After a thirteen-hour flight the aircraft touched down around 4:30 p.m., just as the sun was

9.1 Building the Lion House

9.2 The completed Lion House at the end of the Walkway

setting at Denver International Airport. It was towed into a giant hanger at the United Airlines complex where a crowd of about a hundred people awaited their arrival. The atmosphere was festive, exhibiting the mixture of excitement, anticipation, and anxiety that might befit the arrival of an important personage – or in this case, twenty-five of them.

In addition to the Sanctuary rescue team, there was a huge contingent of cameramen and journalists from a vast array of media outlets, United Airlines and DIA workers, and celebrities and animal welfare activists Bob Barker, of *The Price is Right* fame, and Jorja Fox, who played Sara Sidle on *CSI*, among other roles. The jumbo jet shuddered into place and the pilots cut the engines. When the doors opened to reveal the first of twenty-two custom built lion crates "resounding cheers reminiscent of a world cup event filled the hangar!" Dozens of media cameras flashed. Bob Barker, of course, called out, *"Come on down!!"* And perhaps most significant of all, a chorus of roars exploded from the plane as Bam Bam, Colo Colo, and Dalila, among others, let the waiting throng know that the African lions had most certainly arrived.

9.3 The lions arrive from Bolivia

The crates were inspected by wildlife officials, border control, and drug enforcement agents. Sanctuary animal staff began systematically and efficiently unloading the lions, doing visual health checks, and processing paperwork. After several intensely busy hours, Sanctuary staff loaded the lions carefully onto their transport trailers. The Sanctuary caravan, preceded by many of the media who had left earlier to rush to the observation deck of the new Lion House, began to make its way out of the airport to the outskirts of Keenesburg. Although the twenty-five lions did not know it, they had only thirty miles to go in their 5,000 mile journey home.

The trailers arrived at the Sanctuary at around 10:30 that evening and the painstaking unloading process began. As the night progressed, the lions were released one by one into their new enclosures in the Lion House. Lions are the most social of the big cats and great care was taken to make sure families were kept together and friendships given a chance to develop over the next few weeks and months. Colo Colo and his sisters, Muñeca and Lulu, were the first lions introduced to their new homes. Hercules was ushered into a private "room" but was later reunited with his older daughters, Fida and Panchula. Hercules was also the father of Kiara's cubs, who later would be christened Bob, Percy, and Nancy; they would ultimately be reunited to form a larger pride. The Cavalini Eight lions – king Bam Bam, mother Morena, and their children Campeon, Rosa, Rosita, Rosario, along with two other females, Marta and Maria – had truly left behind the tiny stinking cage in which they had lived for years. Two brothers, Pancho and Temuco, were moved into their own enclosure. Kenya, a younger, rather shy female, would move in with sisters Chitara and Dalila over the next few weeks. India, a quiet but forceful female, preferred her solitude, as did elder statesman Kimba, notable for his calm and composed demeanor.

The media and visitors were waiting eagerly as the crate doors were opened and the lions were released. Many walked cautiously and gingerly across the enclosures, carefully inspecting their newly sodded homes. Imagine encountering spiky, tickling blades of grass between pads accustomed to a lifetime of nothing but unforgiving metal or concrete. After a time, however, caution gave way to exuberance. Colo Colo, Muñeca and Lulu began to leap, bounce, and dash around their new home. Other lions shortly followed suit. Greeting each other with lion head bumps, they rubbed against the pine trees, explored the fencing, and finally collapsed on the soft sod and called it a night. As the media and guests took their leave, Sanctuary staff lowered the lights in the Lion House and bid their new charges good night.

Over the next few months, the Bolivian – now Colorado – lions were tasked with the job of eating their fill, stretching their limbs, becoming acquainted with their neighbors, resting to their hearts' content, and doing whatever they pleased whenever it pleased them. If they wanted to play, they played. If they wanted to eat, they ate. If they wanted to sleep, they slept. For the Sanctuary staff, however, the work was just getting started.

9.4 Sisters Chitara and Dalila out for the night

Casey Craig and a team of staff and volunteers began building outdoor "patios" next to each of the eight interior enclosures on the east and west sides of the Lion House. These exterior pens provided the lions secure outdoor spaces during their acclimation to the immense Colorado prairie. The team also began setting posts and running fence, carving the eighty acres into four enormous habitats that would ultimately become home to the lion prides. They also built underground dens and elevated spool structures for playing and lounging.

Pat and the animal caregivers also began to conduct more thorough medical exams. Chitara had been diagnosed with cataracts, Kimba also was beset with eye problems, and Campeon, with his crooked front legs, was suffering from metabolic bone disease brought on by malnourishment. The females were given Deslorelin implants to prevent any unwanted pregnancies. In other species, the Sanctuary routinely neuters its male rescues. Male lions, however, lose their manes when neutered. Because the mane is an important component of lion identity and a strong indicator of health, male lions are kept intact, and the females are given contraceptive implants.

Teams of dentists from the Peter Emily International Veterinary Dental Foundation (PEIVDF) dealt with the lions' moderate to significant dental problems. The intensive dental care afforded to all the Sanctuary's residents is covered in more detail in a later chapter, but anyone who has ever had a toothache will cringe at the thought of the major oral procedures and oral surgeries needed by the Bolivian lions. Broken teeth, rotten teeth, missing teeth, and the root canal therapies and extractions needed to address the above were the most common problems and procedures conducted in the Sanctuary clinic. Think about how much a toothache hurts (and how much all us complain about it) and then transfer that experience to a 500-pound lion who can do nothing about the pain and has no way of telling anyone about it. Then think of Colo Colo.

If Colo Colo was ill-tempered, he had good reason to be. As Dr. Peter Emily recalled, Colo Colo "had suffered from a broken canine for some time, judging by the size of the canal. The infection was horrible, and the foul-smelling material filling the canal was unbelievable. It is no wonder Colo Colo was in a bad mood." While hardly pleasant to think about, the reality of Colo Colo's pain and his inability to communicate his suffering is heartbreaking. Remarkably, after his root canal therapy within a week of his arrival, Colo Colo began putting on weight and a magnificent, relaxed, and even playful lion began to emerge.

9.5 Colo Colo

Within a short month or two, the lions had gained weight and muscle and were growing into majestic creatures. Meanwhile, the animal care team kept the enrichment toys and games coming, helped by a blanket of snow in early April. Watching the reaction of the lions to this novel weather phenomenon was a delight for all. They sniffed it, ate it, rolled around in it and as their confidence grew chased each other through it. They might have built a snowman if someone could have shown them how!

Each of the prides were released in new habitats that spring and summer. As documented in *The Bolivian Lion Journal* written by Monica Craig and Becca Miceli, each pride spent days and weeks exploring their new homes, watching as the grizzlies next door emerged from hibernation and checking out the tigers in the habitats to the south. They chased tumbleweeds and butterflies, hid amidst the rapidly growing grass to

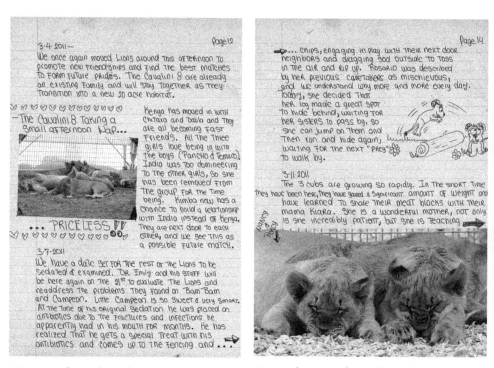

9.6 A page from *The Bolivian Lion Journal* by Monica Craig and Becca Miceli documenting the lions' first year at the Sanctuary

9.7 Another page from *The Bolivian Lion Journal*

pounce on unsuspecting lion-passers-by, and as the weather grew warmer sought the cool repose of their dens.

Over the months that followed, each pride developed its own personality and preferences. As Monica and Becca observed, in the heat of the late summer "Hercules' family has decided they love watching everyone from the top of their den and almost always fall asleep in a neat little line across its crest. Colo Colo and the girls are rarely seen…except for a random head poking out of the den once in a while. Pancho and Temuco's group is usually asleep under their shade structure, with only a tail flick here and there. The Cavalini pride is widely dispersed amongst the levels of their spool structure, with a random leg or two hanging down here and there as they slumber in a cat-a-tonic state."

We sometimes wonder what the sleeping lions dream about. We hope they dream of butterflies and tumbleweeds, falling snow and spring green rains, and the peace of their forever home amidst the comfort and company of family and friends. We imagine them settling comfortably in the Sanctuary, their new "Field of Dreams." Perhaps Hercules might have turned to Kiara, or Bob to Percy, and asked, "Is this heaven?" And the other replied, "No, it's Colorado."

9.8 Brothers Bob and Percy, at 2½ years of age, relaxing during the summer of 2013

9.9 Brothers Bob and Percy, all grown up

Chapter 10

Welcome Home Forever:
Rehabilitation and Release

If all we did were rescues, if we just rescued these animals and then took them to another sanctuary...we wouldn't do it. Because the most daunting thing that you can ever do is go to these places and see the horrific treatment of these animals, the places that they live, the people, and how they treat them. If you had to do that day in and day out it would just get to you and you would shut down...For me going on a rescue is something where I basically put blinders on. I'm not trying to think about how horrific this place is...The little bit that I see outside of my blinders is so horrific. It scars you for life and you remember it... That beautiful lion out there that looks great to you guys? I still have the mental image of where it came from.

These are the words of Casey Craig when we meet for the first time to talk about what it was like to grow up at and dedicate his life's work to The Wild Animal Sanctuary. Since his first rescue when he was ten years old, Casey, Pat Craig's oldest son and the Sanctuary's Chief Operating Officer, has been on dozens of such missions over the years. Some may seek to romanticize the Sanctuary's rescues. Jetting lions and tigers from tiny islands in the Pacific Ocean. The adrenalin-powered jolt of a twenty-two hour drive to Georgia. The heady excitement of a no-knock confiscation raid with armed police. The self-assurance that comes from knowing how to deftly maneuver a one-ton bear into a transport crate. The media frenzy surrounding the arrival of twenty-five lions from Bolivia. But Casey's words sound a cautionary note. Yes, Sanctuary rescues may be dramatic and thrilling but they can be equally horrifying, and the worst of them affect the rescuers – with heartbreak, rage, and despair. Ryan Clements, Director of Operations, concurs, "I know it's a job and what I have to do. I'm ready for anything that could happen. Sometimes the marshals are there. You are always on edge. You do not trust the people and then you see the animals. We get it done. We get out of there as quickly as we can. On the drive back you just decompress and then the images just play back. Everything you saw. That drive back is probably the worst for me...It weighs on me."

And yet, what we see at the Sanctuary is that the rescuers embody an almost limitless passion and resolve to do the tough missions. To stop the suffering. To save just one more animal. It is the tenacious determination of Pat, Casey, Becca, Ryan, Kent and the entire team that most clearly exemplifies the Sanctuary's motto, "Saving one animal may not change the world... but surely, for that one animal, the world will change forever!" The rescue teams keep going, not for the heroics, but for the healing that follows. Casey has seen the hell where these animals come from; he knows the heaven on earth that awaits them here. To Ryan, "The biggest gift is seeing animals I rescued five, six, seven years ago and seeing them now. Now they are turning into who they should be. Seeing a bear or tiger that has never seen another bear or tiger. They are a bear now. Now, they are a tiger." The rescuers know if they can get the animal back to the Sanctuary safely – and in the most harrowing cases, alive – that animal's life will change for the better, because, as Pat puts it, the Sanctuary is "the place where bad beginnings become fantastic futures."

Crossing Thresholds, Changing Lives

Although the big cats and bears hardly realize it, when their transport cages cross the threshold into the Sanctuary trailer, they traverse a threshold from their old life to a new life, and from misery to hope. The healing process begins when Sanctuary team members quietly introduce themselves to the distressed animals. It continues while cages are secured to the walls of the temperature controlled vehicle. Some animals are so relieved to be leaving gruesome circumstances, perhaps enjoying a clean bed for the first time in their lives, that they settle down immediately. Others are more agitated. But one by one, the animals begin to relax in the safety and comfort of the trailer. Soon the rhythmic vibrations of the road and dark solace of true refuge lull the occupants to sleep.

Once the rescued animal arrives at the Sanctuary, rehabilitation begins in earnest. The team of animal caregivers and veterinary staff is keenly attuned to the behavioral norms of different species of large carnivores.

But their deep understanding of normative large carnivore behavior is balanced by an enormous sensitivity to each *individual* animal's preferences and idiosyncrasies. Rehabilitation is carefully tailored to each new resident. Pat and the team consider what they know about an animal's history, but focus mainly on studying its overall demeanor, curiosity or aloofness, interest or disinterest in the activities around it, and other subtleties that provide clues to what makes it tick. They will come to know each animal as well as you do your husband, children, roommates, parents, pets, and any other family or friends you live with day in and day out.

The overall aim, Pat summarizes, is "to prepare our rescued animals so they can transition from previous lives of severe confinement into...large natural spaces with others of their own kind." The rehabilitation process revolves around three main areas: "the physical health, psychological health and social health of the animal." It can take months or even years to get there.

The first step is to take care of physical problems. Many animals arrive fighting for their lives from serious infections caused by inhumane living conditions. Most need some sort of medical or dental attention. All new arrivals are given a checkup by veterinary staff, vaccinated, and administered medications as needed. To prevent reproduction, intact males are neutered. If required, the animal is scheduled for a visit to Colorado State University for MRIs or other more intensive diagnostic procedures. Those requiring ongoing veterinary care stay at the on-site clinic until they are well enough to move to other accommodations. Lions and tigers who do not need medical attention but still require observation may be moved to the Lion House or Tiger Roundhouse; there they can be among others of their own kind and meet new friends and possible roommates.

Many rescues have not eaten well in years; some may *never* have been fed a nutritious diet. Black bear Ricki from the ice cream shop subsisted on dog food, as did Leo, Pat's first lion. Asiatic black bear Lily ate, among other food castoffs, moldy bread. Here, the animals begin eating a wholesome diet rich in nutrients and supplements. Ribs disappear. Muscle tone returns. They rest in solitude. They begin to heal. Cuts and bruises slowly fade. Torn pads mend. Lameness eases. Arthritis medications relieve the pain of joints stiffened by a lifetime of living on concrete. The shine returns to their coats. The light comes back into their eyes and they begin to absorb the activity around them. They start to recognize their caregivers and, hearing their names called out repeatedly, they begin to enjoy the chatter and the attention.

As terrible as the physical problems may be, the psychological scars are often worse. Many animals arriving at the Sanctuary are suspicious or frightened of *everything*. Grass under their feet. The rumble of Sanctuary vehicles. The roar of nearby lions. Other lions and tigers. An open meadow. A big blue sky. An eagle flying overhead. Thunder and lightning. Some have no sense of canid or felid or bruin identity. Tigers arrive at the Sanctuary having never seen another tiger. Lions (the most social of all the big cats) arrive, as Lambert did, not knowing how to roar because they have never been around other lions.

Addressing the psychological scars, the second part of the rehabilitation process, takes time and patience. Fortunately, neurotic, stress-related behaviors typically decrease over time once the animal is living in a healthy environment. Rescued animals are slowly introduced to larger habitats. With most having been confined to small cages, perhaps having never been outside in broad daylight, they need time to adjust to the rich sensory environment of the prairie. Can you imagine how frightening it would be to have lived your entire life in a nine by twelve foot cage and then suddenly be released into a twenty-five acre habitat? To ease the transition, animals are placed in sizable metal transition enclosures called lockouts set within large habitats. Secure within the bounds of this manageable territory, they become accustomed to the ebb and flow of a day at the Sanctuary. They take in the rising and setting of the sun, the birdsong drifting over the land, the scraping of tires on gravel as Sanctuary vehicles make their way around the grounds, the random but regularly spaced meals, the wheeling of gulls, and the roars of lions and howling of wolves. When they are ready, lockout doors are gently opened, and the animals take their first tentative steps toward the greatest freedom they have ever known. Some saunter out of the transition enclosure and slowly and deliberately make their way across the meadow. Others refuse to leave. Mother bears with cubs are notoriously cautious.

In 2016, the Sanctuary rescued twelve bears from an Ohio bear breeding facility. Among them were Molly, a mother grizzly bear with her cub, Betty Jean, and another grizzly, Ersila, with three cubs Scott, Zelda, and Zoll. The cubs were about four months old. Each set of mothers and her cubs were placed in separate transition enclosures within a large habitat and after several weeks of adjustment to their new environs, the doors were opened. Nothing happened. No one moved. Pat describes the scene:

> We knew this was a possibility, since many animals we rescue have lived in very small and confined spaces their whole lives... To them the cold steel walls of their cage represent security and help define their territory, so it's difficult to adapt to a new set of standards overnight. What usually happens is they slowly begin to venture outside their doorway and make little trips; maybe just a few feet into the larger space and then quickly return to safety within their cage where they can contemplate the experience without the pressure of being exposed. These trips begin to get longer and tend to increase in frequency until one day they finally go far enough from their introduction cage to discover one of the underground dens or one of the other man-made amenities we provide them...Once they realize there are plenty of dens and ponds, logs, bear toys, they forget about their old cages and begin enjoying the habitats on a full time basis.

Cubs are generally more enthusiastic about this new and exciting world than are their more protective mothers, and that was the case here. Betty Jean and her mother, Molly, were the first to begin exploring the habitat. Soon they discovered the water tank where they splashed about with great abandon. The other mother, Ersila, eventually began to venture out a few feet with Scott, Zelda, and Zoll. But when the cubs "would start running around like little kids in a Walmart Store...Ersila would blow a

10.1 Bear cubs discover the pool

fuse and gather them up and head back home." This behavior continued for a few days until one day Scott found the water tank and then it was game on! With the whole family splashing about, swimming became part of the daily trek, along with longer jaunts into their new bear "wilderness" until both families were comfortable in their new surroundings.

The third part of the rehabilitation process addresses the social side of each wild animal. We, like many first-time visitors, were surprised to see groupings of animals at the Sanctuary that would never be seen in the wild – or at most zoos for that matter. Here, such tenets as lions live in prides with only one or two males or tigers are notoriously solitary are set aside to accommodate unusual friendships. The circumstances at the Sanctuary and the unusual backgrounds of its captive-born inhabitants simply dictate otherwise. Four magnificent African lions – Cana, Dian, Leo, and Leon – amicably reside together along with three lionesses, Gala, Zoya and Zinna. More than a dozen black bears live harmoniously in a large habitat at the southwest corner of the Walkway. Next door are six tigers who seem to be constantly on the move, swimming in their pond, striding a tall berm, or chasing cars along the driveway. A half dozen foxes cavort in a picturesque habitat alongside the Walkway. Perhaps the most unusual family is comprised of another African lion, also named Leo, and two tigers, Budahshay and Bailey. Pat does not normally mix species in the same habitat, but these three friends grew up together and now live comfortably together on thirty-five acres at The Wild Animal Refuge. At one point, the southernmost meadow at the Sanctuary was occupied by seven camels (six Bactrian and one Dromedary, the beloved Morrison), a herd of yaks, a couple of horses, and a lone emu. It was a veritable United Nations of species whose forebears originated from Central Asia, Northern Africa, Europe, the Americas, and Australia, all living peacefully under the great big Colorado sky.

How is it possible, we wondered, to combine so many wild animals together in single habitats? For starters, the males are neutered (again, except for the African lions), which obviates any rivalry for females. Secondly, there is more than enough food to go around and space to move around in, so there is no competition for sustenance or territory as there would be in the wild. Finally, many of the animals now living together are siblings or grew up together and have worked out genial and sustainable relationships over time.

But the most important factor is the socialization process Pat has honed over decades. He is a master at putting together lion prides and wolf packs, not to mention clusters of tigers, jaguars, leopards, and various other species. His is not a formulaic practice; it relies on keen observation, patience, and a deep understanding not only of species behavioral norms but, even more importantly, individual character and temperament. Many animals at the Sanctuary discover, for the first time, the simple comfort of companionship.

By observing closely the very first animals he rescued, Pat began to develop an understanding of individual and group behavior, "Each one was a little different, some were much more confident, some more fearful. It wasn't necessarily that the abused ones were more fearful. It really boiled down to personality." He continues, "I have always said that is the number one thing – every animal is just like a person, their own background, their own history. So when you are putting together a pride of lions or a group of tigers, that's exactly what you are looking for...the mix that is going to create a nice balance."

It then becomes a matter of watching for little breakthroughs and subtle signs that a positive relationship is developing. Once Pat and the caregivers have a sense of a newer rescue's personality, he or she might be carefully introduced to others of its species. Age, health, and individual history as well as disposition are all taken into consideration. Think of your friends and acquaintances. Some are noisier; others are especially quiet. Some like to party; others would prefer to curl up with a good book. Some are studious, others gregarious. Some are messy and others are neatniks. Some you might enjoy a dinner out with every few months. Others you could live with for the rest of your life. So it goes with the animals at the Sanctuary.

Initial introductions take place behind the safety of adjacent fenced enclosures. Cucho is placed next to Simba in the Tiger Roundhouse; before long they are snuggling up next to each other along the fence. In the Lion House, female lions Mia and Aruzy, rescued from Mexico, are placed in enclosures on either side of Gus, who came to the Sanctuary from Montreal, in hopes of starting a new pride. Buddy, a mountain lion, moves in alongside CeCe, Felix, Montana, and Hunter; Hunter has been here a while and is an enormous help in getting Buddy settled into his new surroundings. Wolves Raven, Yukon, Bridger, and Keona are organized into two groups in an introduction area to see if a larger pack might come together. Lionesses Willa and Uma are introduced to handsome Diablo, one of the lions from Spain, in a comfortable lockout so they can adjust to their new surroundings and so caregivers can observe potential compatibilities.

If the chuffs of tigers, the grunts and moans of lions, and the plaintive woofs of wolves indicate blossoming friendships, the acquaintances are given the opportunity to move in together.

As the most sociable of the big cats, African lions naturally organize themselves into prides, an evolved model for survival in the ecosystems where they thrive. Tight knit, hierarchical family groupings are instrumental in not only hunting large prey animals, such as zebras or wildebeests, on vast savannahs but in defending the kill against other predators. Pat has found that the social dimension is so ingrained in African lions that even those who have always lived in isolation, will naturally gravitate toward family living. Putting a pride together, however, takes time, skill, and tenacity – and we were fascinated by what Pat told us about the process.

The first step is to move potential new pride members next to each other in the Lion House or to place one or two lions in lockouts within a larger lion habitat. At first suspicious of one another, potential new pride members become acquainted behind separate fences, where they can safely work out the dynamics of pride hierarchy – and which they often do in fierce and visceral ways. Pat describes the scenario, "Lions are so physical. They want to hit the fence. We let them get it out...Then at some point, one of the lions goes, 'okay, I'm not going to put in as much time and effort.' He is not the winner; he is the one who is willing to be second rather than first. Those are the clues I'm looking for."

In time, challenges to the pecking order are worked out. When one or more new lions are ready to be released together, Pat and other select team members drive Sanctuary vehicles into the habitat. From the safety of the cabs they open the doors of the lockouts and observe the newcomers' interactions with the rest of the pride. "A whole succession of things happens," Pat explains:

The king will come over first. Then the next highest one in the hierarchy comes over, then the next, until you get to the ones who are peers. They will come over and talk...Then the ones that are below will come over and the new lion will start being bolder but if he gets too tough the king will come over and say, 'I don't want you to get too cocky thinking you can make someone submit in my pride without my permission.' And once that is done, they do it over and over every few hours until it is less and less frequent and finally, they don't do it anymore...But it has to happen multiple times.

If the lions begin to get too rough – and some roughhousing is just about guaranteed – merely driving a van toward the scuffle will often be enough to distract them. But, in fact, the openness of the enormous habitat tends to tamp down any antagonistic behavior. Pat shakes his head, "Lions are like two guys in a bar fight who act aggressively when people are restraining them and then when they are let go, they're like, 'oh, okay.' So with the fence they can act way tougher than when you let them out in the open. There is not nearly as much bravado or physicality when they are finally together." But Pat is the first to admit, "it can be scary to watch....The lions will do a lot of smacking and hitting so you learn to look past the bravado and look for the real details. Is it really serious? Or is it just loud?

As the pride comes together group dynamics continue to evolve. Some lions will be more protective of lesser pride denizens, barring assertive members of the family from pushing them around. Those with more playful and gregarious natures help the newcomers come out of their shells. Each of the members has strengths and weaknesses and unique traits that combine to define the pride – just like any other family.

10.2 Lionesses at the Sanctuary

Every species has its own set of social norms. The process of putting wolves together, who naturally gravitate toward packs, is similar to that for lions. As Pat says about the wolves, "You give them a hundred acres, they are going to come together and live together because it's in their genes. It wouldn't matter how big the space is, they are going to do it." By contrast, while tigers may willingly live together, they are more roommates than families. They tend to need more solitude and privacy, which is why enormous habitats are so beneficial to tiger well-being. As for bears, if they have enough food, they are happy. Pat laughs, "Their whole life is about food. They love food. They don't eat to survive the way other animals do; they just *love* food." If there is enough food – and there is at the Sanctuary – the bears will go along to get along.

All in all, it takes a tremendous amount of time and commitment to bring animals together in groups – an effort that many other zoos or sanctuaries are unwilling or unable to make. "Of course," Pat says, "we never force any animals to live together." Different species and individual animals have their preferences and their boundaries, distinct needs for personal space and for sociable companionship. Pat and the team may offer the opportunity, but the animals decide.

When Big Cats Go to the Dogs

The Sanctuary does not breed, of course; no true Sanctuary does. But that does not mean that young animals are completely out of the picture. Sometimes the Sanctuary is informed about possible pregnancies, as in the cases of O.B. and Ursula, the grizzly bears from Georgia. Other times, an unexpected package from the stork surprises everyone. The Sanctuary goes to great lengths to keep mothers and cubs together; in fact, the family may live together for the better part of their lives.

The toughest situations are when rescues bring with them orphaned cubs. Without the protection of their mother, a big cat or bear cub is too vulnerable to join an adult group. They are nurtured by Sanctuary staff, but they also benefit tremendously from animal companionship. That is often when the dogs come into play.

There have always been dogs in Pat's life. Not surprisingly, most have been rescues. English bulldogs, boxers, two pint-sized pooches Marcel and Little Bit, massive Komondors, and of course, the giants of the dog world, Irish Wolfhounds. When the Sanctuary moved to Keenesburg, Pat relates, "People constantly dumped dogs." There were no houses nearby. The Sanctuary was surrounded by dirt roads. People would drive up and push the dogs out of their trucks. For a while Pat was finding stray dogs two or three times a month; he and his family would find good homes for them. But they kept some of the dogs and took in other rescues. Butchie the Bulldog was about to be euthanized when the vet called Pat about taking him in. Little Bit was found wandering in Keenesburg. The first Wolfhounds came from a woman in Brighton who had a litter of eight and could not get rid of them. Pat ended up with two nine-month old puppies tipping the scales at about one hundred pounds each. Then Sanctuary visitors started calling, saying they had seen the Wolfhounds and asking if Pat would like a few more. Matilda had a badly broken front leg. One of the orthopedic surgeons from CSU was called in to see what he could do; Matilda still runs on it today. Monica Craig drove to Nevada for a Wolfhound. Another came from Illinois.

Of course, everyone at the Sanctuary has a job to do and the dogs are no exception. Over the years, a variety of dogs have been drafted into taking care of orphaned cubs. Judah, a mountain lion youngster, played with Dave, a bulldog mix. Eddy, the black leopard cub, also grew up with bulldogs.

In 2015 Canadian Fish and Wildlife officers called about two six-week old African lion cubs who had been owned by a drug dealer and seized in a drug raid. In honor of the *Canadian* Ministry of Environment whose staff worked diligently to find the cubs a new home, Sanctuary staff christened them Cana (pronounced Cane) and Dian (pronounced Dee-on). Once back at the Sanctuary, Nellie, Butchie and other members of the dog pack began acting as pseudo-siblings to the small cubs. Pat paints a vivid picture, "The dogs raised Cana and Dian, two gigantic lions now. They did everything the dogs did. If the dogs got in the truck, they got in the truck...We made sure they ate right but the dogs just said

10.3 Lioness cub Gala and Labrador Petey

10.4 Big dog and big cat naptime

you are one of us and took care of them and played with them." Finally, at about 200 pounds, Cana and Dian were big enough and strong enough to go in with the other lions – which is the whole point of dog pack interventions.

Today Cana and Dian live with lions Leo and Leon and lionesses Zoya and Zinna, all rescued from Ohio, and lioness Gala. In part due to its proximity to the Walkway and the commanding and unusual presence of four stunning male lions lounging about together, this pride is one of the signature families of the Sanctuary. On hot summer days, they are often found lying in a companionable heap under one of the shade canopies in the vast meadow.

10.5 The Cana, Dian, Leo, Leon pride

Nothing Like Six Months of Good Night's Sleeps

As anyone of us can attest to, there is nothing like a good night's sleep. And if you are a bear, there is nothing so healing or rejuvenating as about six months of good night's sleeps. Hibernation is a miraculous process which, for bears, is as normal as breathing. A brilliant solution for species survival, hibernation keeps bears alive during brutally cold and snowy winters when there is little or no food available for these foragers. When winter sets in, bears are simply programmed to sleep.

Yet, the hibernation process often has been cruelly thwarted for bears rescued by the Sanctuary. Lacking the robust health, ample diet, seasonal weather changes, and access to cozy dens they need to hide away for the winter, many rescued bears have *never* hibernated. So, giving them the tools they need to hibernate is a crucial part of the bear rehabilitation process.

Hibernation in bears is a multi-step process that goes something like this. The bear transitions from normal summer activity to hyperphagia (a tremendous increase in appetite) in late summer, to a fall transition period, to hibernation in winter, and finally, walking hibernation as it emerges from its den in the spring. Hyperphagia triggers a gorging period where the bear eats and drinks excessively. A grizzly can easily consume more than 20,000 calories a day and put on more than twenty pounds in a week. Sanctuary animal caregivers feed a vast smorgasbord of summer and fall harvested fruits and vegetables, roast chickens, fish and shellfish, cakes and doughnuts, and everything else that suits a ravenous omnivore – which is almost anything.

During the fall transition period the bear's metabolic system slows down. While the bear continues to drink large amounts of water, it eats less. It starts hanging around its den, sleeping as much as twenty-two hours a day. The bruin finally succumbs to severe lethargy and the lure of the den and settles in for the winter. Although each differs in terms of behavior and timing, most of the Sanctuary's 200-plus bears are tucked into their dens by Thanksgiving. That is when the wondrous physiological feat known as hibernation begins.

During the big sleep, a bear's metabolism slows by as much as twenty-five to fifty percent. Its normal heart rate of forty to fifty beats per minute drops to a mere eight to nineteen beats per minute. Breathing slows dramatically. Normal respiration rates are six to ten breaths per minute compared to one breath every forty-five seconds during hibernation. Body temperature is maintained at around ninety degrees. A misconception about hibernation is that the animals are in such a deep sleep they never move. Not so. A bear will sleepily roll over and change position, yawn, stretch, fluff up the bedding, or scratch an itch during its six-month or longer hibernation period. It may wake up to defend itself if something or someone is foolish enough to wander into its den. A bear may even wander out of its den in mid-winter if a few days of warmer weather hint at a false spring. At the Sanctuary, it is not unusual to see a bear or two strolling around when temperatures hit the 50s or 60s for a few days. Jake, the great Kodiak, could be seen hanging around the front porch of his den in February, but once he realized there was no food forthcoming, he would head back inside to hit the hay.

The most implausible aspect of a bear's hibernation is that even though the animal is not taking in any food or water, it stays healthy by living off its fat. As fat tissues break down, they release water, which keeps the bear nicely hydrated. Plus bears utilize urea, a component of urine, and essentially recycle it to produce new protein. In hibernation a bear will burn 4,000 calories a day and can lose thirty percent of its body weight. But it feels no long term deleterious effects from its six-month diet. Humans would suffer from nutritional deficiencies, diabetes, kidney failure, high cholesterol, muscle cramping, or bone density problems. Not so the bear. As Pat exclaims, "Bears are awesome! Bears are the only animal that I know of that can eat insane amounts of sugar and it never hurts them. It does not hurt their organs. They do not get clogged arteries. They do not have high blood pressure. In the wild they eat all these sweet berries in the fall, and they convert sugar to fat…So the more sugar they get the better… We would all love to have a system like that!" Yes, we would – which is among the reasons that molecular and evolutionary biologists continue to study hibernation and its possible genetic and biological applicability to human health, and even space travel.

Consistently warmer temperatures rouse the big bruins from their long winter's naps; at the Sanctuary, most bears have emerged by the end of April. During the first few weeks, the bear goes through a two- to three-week period known as walking hibernation. Metabolic processes begin to return to normal. The bears begin drinking water and nibbling on grass and small amounts of food. Eventually all systems return to normal and bears eagerly line up at the Sanctuary buffets!

Seeing firsthand the refreshing and therapeutic quality of hibernation drives home the inhumanity of depriving a bear of what it needs to thrive. It is thrilling to witness newly arriving bears hibernate for the first time *ever*! During the summer of 2018, grizzly bears Atze, age 22, and Barolina, age 24, arrived from Buenos Aires, where the temperature rarely dips below fifty degrees in the winter. Hibernation was not really on their radar screens. In the fall, instinct kicked in and they began eating more and taking to their dens for longer and longer naps, eventually disappearing until spring when they emerged rejuvenated and ready to go. Even bears who are well cared for by zoos are often not allowed to hibernate, amid concerns that the paying public might complain. Polly, a big brown bear, and Migwan, a small North American black bear, were brought to the Sanctuary from the Detroit Zoo when it decided to reduce its bear population. Accompanied to the Sanctuary by concerned and caring zookeepers, the two girls were for the first time ever able to enjoy a true hibernation in comfy underground dens. Then there is Lily, a female Asiatic black bear rescued from a Maryland roadside zoo in the fall of 2016.

"Lily," Pat laughs, "was the biggest, fattest bear I have ever seen." The zoo owner had placed Lily in a filthy twelve-foot diameter corn crib a decade earlier as a cub – and had never let her out. Not only did she have no place to hibernate, the dirt floor was mud-slicked and puddled from rains and feeble attempts on the part of the owner to wash away Lily's feces. She was fed "ground corn, dog food, or other cheaply-acquired grains" supplemented by "bags of leftover food filled with stale donuts, onions, and moldy bread" left at the end of the driveway by well-meaning locals. In her tiny cage, all Lily could do was "wallow around in a small circle," lay in mud and manure, and eat and eat and eat. Visitors noticed two massive growths under her belly. As public concern grew over these potentially malignant tumors, PETA, the USDA, and local animal control finally brought enough pressure on the owner and he agreed to surrender Lily. An examination by Sanctuary veterinarians revealed that the two massive growths were not tumors at all but rather "extensive secondary fat storage pockets." Lily was several hundred pounds overweight and suffering from morbid obesity.

10.6 Lily in her former cage – and at her former weight

Pat knew that eating a healthier diet and living in a large acre habitat where she could stroll, run, play, and swim would help Lily shed the pounds. But "the best option coming down the pike...was that Lily would be able to hibernate!" The regimen worked. Between the new diet and hibernation Lily lost more than 200 pounds. Lily is a shadow of her former self and, with a round of dental work to clean and repair her teeth, she revels in her ability to walk to and from the buffet freely, easily, and without the encumbrance of obesity.

10.7 Lily at the Sanctuary

Recently, Lily has been joined by Dillan, also an Asiatic black bear who holds the dubious distinction of having surpassed Lily as "the biggest, fattest bear" Pat had ever seen. If Lily was fat, Dillan was even fatter, an estimated 300 to 350 pounds overweight!

Dillan had spent ten years at a Pennsylvania gun club where he was caged in a small chain link enclosure adjacent to the club's shooting range. Constantly stressed by the unceasing report of high powered rifles Dillan engaged in almost nonstop stereotypic rocking. He also was hideously obese and aching from painfully infected teeth and gums that were in danger of becoming septic and life threatening. Dillan's plight gained widespread attention after PETA challenged the gun club to alleviate the bear's horrible suffering and the USDA began issuing citations to the owners. When the public got behind the rescue, the gun club finally acquiesced. "I have rarely seen more people get engaged with a captive animal in need of rescue than people did with Dillan," explained Brittany Peet from the PETA Foundation. In January 2020, a rescue team headed to Pennsylvania to collect the Sanctuary's newest bear resident.

Dillan's obesity really hit home when it took twelve strong and able staff to lift the bear's gurney, but only about eight inches off the ground! Kent Drotar wryly noted that upon arriving at the Sanctuary, Dillan tried out a brand new fire hose hammock made for the Sanctuary by local Eagle Scouts – and the straps held! Kent smiles, "We got it the day before Dillan arrived, on Monday" and his great bulk "could be the best test you could ever have for it."

The team looks forward to seeing Dillan go through the same amazing transformation as did Lily. Although declawed on all four feet, he is already moving slowly around his large habitat and eating a healthier diet. Dillan will enjoy his first hibernation ever this coming winter and should emerge a more svelte and much healthier bear in the spring.

10.8 Dillan at the Sanctuary

It is fascinating to watch Sanctuary bears go through the stages of hibernation over the course of a year. Their disappearance by Thanksgiving heralds the holidays. Their deep sleep in January and February signals that winter is a time for all of us to draw close to the fire and do a little cozy hibernating ourselves. Their emergence in the spring is cause for celebration, a sense that the earth is renewing itself. Modern life is wound tightly by the clock; the Sanctuary's beloved bears draw us back into the cycle of the seasons and the cycle of life.

Chapter 11

🐾 🐾 🐾 🐾 🐾 🐾 🐾 🐾 🐾 🐾 🐾 🐾 🐾 🐾 🐾 🐾
🐾 🐾 🐾 🐾 🐾 🐾 🐾 🐾 🐾 🐾 🐾 🐾 🐾 🐾 🐾 🐾

Do Fence Me In:
Habitats and Housing at the Sanctuary

R yan Clements and the operations team have built a parthenon on the
prairie. The original Parthenon is a gleaming white marble temple
situated on the Acropolis high above the city of Athens and dedicated to
Athena, the patron goddess and namesake of the city. The prairie parthenon
is a rustic telephone pole and timber temple located in a sweeping meadow
just west of the Bear Deck; it looks rather like what might happen if a Greek
temple met a Rocky Mountain cabin. Constructed with a low pitched roof
built of interlocking timbers set on a ridge beam, it has seven tall columns
across the front and six along the sides. The shade and play structure has
plenty of climbing spaces and platforms for lounging, which is perfect
because the Sanctuary parthenon is a temple for tigers – specifically, four
young tigers named Clay, Daniel, Enzo, and Thomas who were rescued
from Joe Exotic's roadside zoo in Oklahoma. Since coming to the Sanctuary
about two years ago, the four tigers have been living in a habitat well east
of the Walkway. They will move to the "tiger temple" habitat in February
and Becca Miceli has invited us to watch the move from the adjacent Bear
Deck. We make plans to be there.

Of course, planning any outdoor activity in Colorado in February can be
iffy, to say the least. Temperatures may hover around 60 degrees or plummet
to bone-chilling conditions in the teens. Moving day for the four tigers brings
with it the latter; it is sixteen degrees when we arrive at the Sanctuary in the
early afternoon. The sky is the color of a gray woolen sock. The low ceiling
blends and blurs into the snow-washed horizon. Icy squalls are blowing
sideways out of the north, pinging snow against our faces. The Sanctuary
is closed, an extremely rare occurrence, due to inclement weather and icy
conditions. We park our car behind the Carnivore Nutrition Center and walk
carefully up the snow-covered ramp next to the habitat where grizzly bears

Boris, Natasha, and Tiny are deep in winter slumber. We are each wearing the base layer we bought for a cruise to Antarctica a few years ago, turtlenecks, our orange Sanctuary hoodies and heavy Sanctuary jackets, scarves, ski hats, wool socks, and hiking boots. We have stuffed handwarmers into our gloves. We still freeze. We spend a few minutes on the Bear Deck but with no sign yet of the trailer carrying the tigers, we gingerly make our way back down the ramp. We sit in the car with the heater fan cranked up full tilt. Before our feet have fully thawed, Becca texts that they are on the way and we once more head up the ramp. Joined by Communications Director and Pat's wife Monica Craig, who is carrying a camera with an impressive zoom lens, we chat, we wait, we all freeze together.

11.1. The tigers arrive at their new "tiger temple"

The animal care crew below us seems oblivious to the weather as they quickly open gates and undertake last minute preparations for the new residents. The operation is smooth, fast, and efficient. Ryan maneuvers the Dodge truck and gooseneck trailer through the gate and circles around in front of the wood structure, tires crunching on the frozen ground. Becca and animal caregiver Stacey Morse follow him in a white van. Becca waves cheerfully to us as Ryan backs a forklift out of the back of the trailer. One by one, Ryan forklifts the transport cages containing the tigers out of the vehicle and places them side by side in the snow.

Daniel crouches in the first cage; he is enormous. The other three boys, Enzo, Thomas, and Clay sit or stand, wary and waiting. Because the four tigers have been living together in a large habitat, they will be released into the expansive meadow rather than spending orientation time in lockouts. The forklift is loaded back into the trailer and Becca drives the assembly out of the habitat. The habitat's double gates are secured.

It takes only a few seconds to release the big cats. Becca, Ryan, and Stacey quickly unlock the secondary chains that secure the cage doors, leaving the door handles in the lock position. They hurry back to the van and Becca drives up to the first cage. Ryan opens the passenger-side window, releases the cage door handle, and sets the door ajar. The van moves to the next cage and the process is repeated. Each tiger steps carefully out of his transport cage and pads quickly across the frozen snow. Daniel heads off alone to the south toward the newly planted trees along the fence line; the others pause, glance around, and head west together. Becca, Ryan, and Stacey will keep watch for a while from the safety and warmth of the van, ensuring the four boys are comfortable in their new surroundings.

11.2 The tigers are released into their new habitat

The neighbors certainly are interested in the newcomers. The wolves just to the south appear mildly alarmed, even though they have lived next to other tigers for quite some time. Ajack begins howling and soon he is joined by a chorus of yowls and wails heralding the arrival of the four big cats. African lions Bob, Percy, and other members of the pride to the north lope briskly over to the fences between the two meadows, interested in giving the strangers a once over. They check to make sure the tigers are carefully secured within the boundaries of their new home and pose no threat of invasion. That is what fences are for, aren't they? They protect your territory from intruders; they keep potential invaders away from your home.

Good Fences Make Good Neighbors

What the wolves and African lions might have been thinking the day that Clay, Daniel, Enzo, and Thomas moved in next door was: Thank heavens we have a fenced-in home! We do not have to worry about being bothered by these new neighbors! But why would a lion or wolf want to be fenced in? Don't all wild animals yearn to be free? Aren't they all trying to escape from their enclosures? Don't all these animals hate the fences that keep them from going where they want to go? The answer is quite simply, no.

Consider the mindset of "captive" wild animals as opposed to "wild" wild animals. Large carnivores born and raised in captivity are quite distinct behaviorally and psychologically from those who live in the wild. The Sanctuary's rescues have a completely different perspective on "wild life," as it were. The lions know nothing about African savannahs, grizzly bears nothing about the wilds of Alaska, and tigers nothing about the jungles of India. These animals have always been held in captivity. They have never learned to hunt. Theirs is a world of enclosures where food is delivered, not chased on the hoof. Captive-born big cats and bears may not be any less dangerous than their wild counterparts but having never had the freedom to roam in natural habitats, they see fences as a source of safety and security. As Pat has explained, "Captive wildlife believe the fencing and enclosures they live in are designed to keep others out – rather than holding them in. They see fences as barriers that help keep them safe from others who might want to threaten their lives or invade their territory." To captive large carnivores, the fences are there for them, not for us. Of course, we know they are there for us, too. But that is not how the animals see it, especially since their habitat homes are enormous and engaging.

Large carnivore habitats have come a long way in the forty years since Pat started the Sanctuary in 1980. USDA regulations at the time required that the big cats and bears be housed in roughly 500-square-foot enclosures. Chain link was the material of choice for walls and roofs; the floors were concrete. In building his large carnivore compound, Pat became increasingly frustrated with what he considered to be unnecessary enclosure requirements, until he found an "out:"

I'm helping these animals, but now they are stuck in these crappy cages. So the first thing I did was reread the regulations and realized there was a loophole. You could take animals out to do their work, like going into a ring at a circus. As long as they were safely contained, they could be out of their normal cage. The regulations dictated cage size but didn't say anything about the size of the exercise area or performance area. So I started to take them out and let them run on the fifteen acres...It definitely made me feel a lot better.

So, thirty-six years ago Pat began building acre-sized habitats, eventually splitting the family farm into three fenced areas where he could let the big carnivores out during the day and gather them up again at night, all in compliance with then-current USDA rules.

Over the years the CPW and the USDA began to change some of their fencing and animal management requirements on a case-by-case basis. Pat was thus able to leave the big cats and bears outside day and night rather than ushering them into their small pens in the evening. As the Sanctuary moved to larger properties and as Sanctuary acreage grew so did the habitats, opening a new world for the rescued animals. To put that in perspective, Joe Exotic bragged about having more than two hundred tigers – which were kept in twelve by twelve foot cages on a total of sixteen acres. By contrast, at The Wild Animal Sanctuary, each tiger habitat *alone* is about sixteen acres, and each is home to *only* four or five tigers. Pat, who has always thought in terms of acres and not square feet, quite simply raised the bar on animal well-being by committing to the creation of large-scale habitats for his rescued animals.

The problem was that building large habitats for the burgeoning number of rescues was getting to be enormously expensive. It was costly enough just to provide high quality care for the large carnivores. They consumed vast amounts of food, required ongoing veterinary care and periodic medical and dental procedures, as well as prescription medications. If the Sanctuary was going to survive, and thrive, two things had to happen. By the early 1990s, Pat knew he would have to seek donated materials and equipment and, second, he and his small team of volunteers would have to figure out how to build just about everything themselves. It was simply too expensive to have to buy materials and then pay contractor costs.

Since then, chain link fencing, concrete pipes of all sizes, concrete culverts, concrete cisterns, telephone poles, conduit, gutter drain boxes, cable spools, lumber, and even trees have made their way to the Sanctuary, all due to generous donations from various private and public entities and the resourcefulness of Pat and the team. The Sanctuary has always built its own fences, dens, shelters, and play structures, as well as the Tiger Roundhouse, most of the Lion House, the Carnivore Nutrition Center, and more. Staff and volunteers maintain and repair everything from donated trucks and vans to forklifts and fire engines. As Casey Craig puts it, "As a nonprofit, you are asking people to give you their hard-earned money to benefit the animals...we are going to make your $20 donation go a lot farther if we do the work ourselves."

Growing up at the Sanctuary, Casey learned to drive every vehicle and operate every piece of equipment. As a ten-year old kid, he was supervising volunteers in the construction of new habitats. Becca, who started as a volunteer working in animal care and maintenance, went to structural welding school so she could help build cages, the Walkway, and habitats. Volunteers pitched in with maintenance – as they still do today – clearing out tumbleweeds and noxious weeds, repairing fences, painting, cleaning, and participating annually in what is known as the Dig Down, when wood chips are replenished in the Tiger Roundhouse and Lion House. Volunteer Nadine explains, "I love the Dig Down. It is my favorite animal care thing. Twice a year we dig the wet woodchips all the way down to the dirt and bring in new woodchips. When the babies come back out...they love it!" The "can-do" attitude explains how the Sanctuary has been built, maintained, and reconfigured over the years.

Rest and Recreation:
Dens, Watering Holes, and Playgrounds

A tremendous amount of energy is expended by Sanctuary staff and volunteers to make animal habitats as interesting, comfortable, and homey as possible. Over the years, the requisite chain link fences on poles set ten feet apart have been replaced by high tension game fences on telephone poles set twenty feet apart. Game fence, and the hot-wires needed to meet USDA regulations, are among the few major purchases made by the Sanctuary.

The fencing is not nearly as off-putting as chain link "prison" fence and almost disappears against the prairie landscape. Plus, game fences allow animal caregivers to administer medications more easily. Meds are tucked into raw meat that is skewered on the end of a long pole and pushed through the steel grid to the animal waiting for its treat on the other side.

A good many of the habitats are interchangeable, which makes sense since changing circumstances often require moving animals around. Transferring a few bears out and moving a few lions in may entail building some new dens and bringing in spools for climbing in the new lion space, while the bears pack up their tires, balls, and swings as they wave goodbye on the way to their new digs. But there are some habitats that are purpose built for either the species they house or for individual animals who might require a little special attention. The jaguars have a jungle gym, the leopards have a sky bridge, and the mountain lions have fencing that goes far beyond – and above – the typical habitat. As for those individuals needing special attention, the Sanctuary is home to two grizzly bears who, as we will see, live in what may be the premier, if not the only, handicap-accessible habitat for animals in all the world.

If you were asked to create the best possible home for large carnivores, where would you start? We might ask, if you want to build a house, where would you start? With your wish list, of course! You might hope for a kitchen with an island, an open space plan, three bedrooms, two baths, a shaded front porch, a big backyard for the kids and the dogs, and a mudroom for everyone. And you might want a home that is environmentally friendly with solar panels or a green roof, a smaller footprint, and sustainably sourced materials.

Bears, tigers, lions, and other carnivores have different wish lists. Bears might ask for a comfortable and cozy, not-too-large den where they can curl up for their long winter sleeps. Lions and tigers seek sheltering lairs. Some of the smaller animals like lynx and servals find prefab dog igloos to their liking. Tigers love to swim, as do bears. Jaguars and leopards are talented climbers who love the high ground. All the animals at the Sanctuary need shade from the Colorado summer sun and shelter from high winds that race across the plains.

So, when the design teams at the Sanctuary build new habitats for their residents, they think about how each animal might find or build a den in the wild, where and how they like to play, the kind of shelters they will need, and what type of water feature might be most suitable. They also consider natural materials, ergonomics, durability, and weather resistance.

Then they go to work with backhoes, Bobcats, donated pipes, and concrete culverts.

Dens are typically constructed using concrete pipes that are laid end to end to form a roughly forty- to sixty-foot long tunnel. The tunnel rises slightly for about ten feet and then falls downhill the rest of the way, leading to a cozy concrete culvert where the animal sleeps underground. The concrete tunnel and culvert are completely covered with mounds of dirt and rocks that blend with the prairie landscape. The dens are filled with comfy wood chips and straw bedding that is changed out periodically.

Dens are situated well below ground where the temperature stays about sixty degrees year round – a perfect sleeping temperature for big cats and bears – although many of them prefer camping out in the wide open spaces. Casey explains, "If you were to create a den above ground, you would have to temperature-control it somehow which would be a lot more costly. Once you are three feet below ground level it is 60 degrees year round...In the summertime that is a great air conditioner...In the wintertime sixty degrees is plenty warm for these guys. Most of them do not even really utilize the dens that much in the wintertime. They will sleep out when there's two feet of snow out here. We have pictures of whole lion prides sleeping in two feet of snow."

11.3 Entrance to the den

11.4 Tunnel to the underground den

As with everything at the Sanctuary, individual dens are tailored to the animals who will be using them. The concrete pipe at the entrance to Kodiak bear Jake's den measures 12 feet in diameter. But most concrete pipe entrances average about four feet in diameter. Indeed, it can be rather entertaining to stand on the Walkway and wonder if a black or grizzly bear will really be able to maneuver its ample girth through the concrete pipe opening. Yet the small entrance is just the way they like it ("just right" one might say in Goldilocks parlance). In the wild, bears will normally dig dens just big enough to hold them on the northern slopes of mountains; the small entrances become covered with an insulating layer of snow in the winter.

Because the high plains receive only about twelve inches of rain a year, getting enough water to meet the needs of the Sanctuary is a constant challenge. Wells throughout the property provide fresh water and cyclical monsoon rains toward the end of summer help, although heat waves and droughts can tax even the most conscientious water conservationists among us. All the animal habitats are furnished with large drinking water basins. Sizable stock tanks are emptied and refilled with fresh water twice a week. The old water is recycled at the base of the many trees that have been planted around the property over the years.

The stock tanks are perfect for a quick dip on a hot day, or even for a quick dip on a cold day. A tiger will break through six inches of ice to get to the water below.

Some "watering holes" are more elaborate. Ponds made of "shotcrete," a Quickcrete concrete product that is shot out of a high pressure hose onto a waterproof liner, can be customized to the desired size, depth, and shape. Grizzly bears Tiny, Natasha and Boris have a tall waterfall in their Quickcrete pond. It recirculates the water and provides a continual cascade of bubbles that serves as a source of great entertainment for both bears and visitors. Like all brown bears, these three grizzlies are distinguished by a powerful muscled hump across their shoulders and claws longer than a human index finger, which make them prodigious diggers. Pat knew from experience that the bears would be flinging dirt and Quickcrete sky high, so a deeper traditional concrete mixture was poured around the perimeter of the pool to create an eight inch apron strong enough to withstand grizzly excavations.

The jaguar and leopard habitats are two of the most elaborate at the Sanctuary. The jaguar is the largest big cat in the western hemisphere and the third largest in the world, behind tigers and lions. When adjusted for body size, the jaguar has one of the strongest bite forces of any big cat in the world. The leopard is native to sub-Saharan Africa and large swaths of Asia. Golden jaguars and leopards are often confused, but jaguars are bigger-boned, brawnier, heavier, and their rosettes have a central dot. If you are a football fan, think of the jaguar as a tight end (bigger, stronger, beefier) and the leopard as a wide receiver (lithe, agile, and fluid). Both big cats are brilliant and fearless climbers.

Leopards love the high ground, so in 2016 the team built them a sky bridge. The graceful structure crosses a large tree-lined seasonal pond and is suspended between two high towers, which are accessed by two lengthy ramps. Horizontal platforms, an amazing thirty feet above the prairie floor, are situated adjacent to each tower.

Visitors love seeing Jumanji and the other leopards deftly make their way up the angled and suspended ramp (without the benefit of handrails!), lightly spring onto the lofty observation roosts, and settle in to watch the passing scene all the way to the horizon. Ryan smiles at the memory of Jumanji on the suspension bridge between the two towers, "I've seen Jumanji in the middle of the sky bridge. It's pretty windy and it's swaying back and forth and he's just lying there, swinging back and forth." Clearly, there is no fear of heights among these big cats!

11.5 The leopard sky bridge

11.6 Jumanji on the sky bridge ramp

When it was time to create a new jaguar habitat for Manchas and Negrita, Casey and Ryan knew they would have their work – and fun – cut out for them. Jaguars are smart, inquisitive, cunning, and curious. Accordingly, Casey and Ryan created a massive, free-form "jungle gym" hundreds of feet long with ponds and water features below. Casey laughs, "We were like two kids with a bunch of Lincoln Logs thinking what kind of cool stuff can we build for the jaguar play structure. We didn't come up with any plan at all. We just said we're going to start and see what it ends up looking like...we just kept going at it like little kids." The result was a jaguar playset extraordinaire with lofty perches, long log bridges over water, stacked cable spools, and comfy hammocks.

11.7 Jaguar jungle gym

When Eight Feet Just Will Not Do

Basketball legend Michael Jordan, whose athletic prowess earned him the title of "Air Jordan" over his almost twenty-year career, boasted a forty-eight inch vertical leap. Added to his 6'-6" height, this feat enabled him to get his head six inches above the rim of the basket. For Jordan, this combination of leap and height make dunking the ball, well, a slam dunk.

Yet Air Jordan has nothing on Montana, Buddy, Felix, or Kiera, all of whom Pat describes as "tightly wound rubber bands just waiting to explode." Each can jump a staggering fifteen feet high when standing still – almost four times Jordan's best. Plus, they are only about three feet tall to the top of their heads, less than half of Jordan's 6'-6" height. How is this possible? Well, Montana, Buddy, Felix, and Kiera are all mountain lions, the rockets of the wild cat world.

All big cats demonstrate remarkable athletic talents and sheer power, with running and sprinting, jumping, and leaping, and climbing capabilities far beyond our own. Their enviable athleticism is one of the aspirational reasons we name our sports teams after them. Topping out at less than 200 pounds, mountain lions are only about one-third the size of African lions or tigers, yet they can bound up to forty feet when running, scale a twelve foot fence, and hit fifty miles per hour in a sprint. Plus, they can effortlessly leap fifteen or sixteen feet up into a tree from a spring-loaded crouch below.

To thwart their amazing climbing and leaping abilities, rescued mountain lions at the Sanctuary are housed in smaller roofed enclosures. Pat, however, wanted the mountain lions to be able to enjoy larger habitats where they could get up a good run or simply lie in the shade of a tree. Fencing for these energetic acrobats, however, really stumped the operations team. The question was how to build a fence high enough to counteract the amazing vertical leap? The high-tensile steel fences used in other big cat habitats were strong enough but at eight-feet high, not nearly tall enough. High-tensile fences must be stretched and tensioned between poles set at precise distances, which is not a problem at eight feet but would have been impossible at sixteen feet. Even if a second fence could have been placed atop the first, thus reaching the sixteen-foot required height, it would have been impossible to properly tension it.

The team found the answer in zoo netting. Made of stainless steel, zoo netting is strong and will not rust or decay. It does not need to be tensioned, but it is expensive. In 2014, a Colorado foundation provided the funds to create a sizable habitat south of the Tiger Roundhouse. The zoo netting passed the test. Today, when its door is opened by keepers, a mountain lion can leave its smaller enclosure, traverse a chain link tunnel, and run into an open grassy meadow with climbing structures, trees, and Colorado's long range views. The mountain lions are rotated in and out, sometimes singly, other times in pairs.

The shared habitat is a perfect solution for these felids, because mountain lions typically do not stay out all day. Not only are they the great leapers of the big cat world, they also are masters at big cat FOMO; that is, they seem (like many of us) to have a "fear of missing out" on something. So, over the course of a day, they repeatedly return to their enclosures to see what is happening, check on possible food deliveries, and make sure the other mountain lions are not having a good time without them. The mountain lions, like all the animals at the Sanctuary, simply set their own agendas.

11.8 Mountain lion Cascade

Creating a Handicap Accessible Habitat for Walter and Mafalda

We first see grizzly bears Walter and Mafalda during a tour with Kent Drotar. Walter is leaning back against a mound of dirt and Mafalda is sitting in front of him, keeping an eye on her best friend. The Sanctuary rescued both bears (as well as two lions and three tigers) in 2017 from Colon, Argentina where they lived together in a zoo so horrific that it had been identified as one of the ten worst zoos in the world. Although all the animals were in bad shape, Walter was one of the worst. He had been brutally declawed, and his teeth had been ground down to stubs that barely protruded beyond his gum line. Walter was also both blind and deaf. In an amazing display of animal resourcefulness and adaptation, Pat noted, "Walter had mentally mapped his cage and was able to navigate the entire space by memory." Mafalda was equally amazing, for she had assumed the role as Walter's caregiver and protector, carefully guiding him around the space.

The team, having rescued other blind animals over the years, knew Walter would require a specially designed habitat so he could make his way around his new home. They also knew he was smart enough to figure out a new navigational system. So they created a winding path of russet-colored sandstone around the habitat. The path leads from the den to the food buffet, made up of a special diet of fruits, vegetables, and other soft and nutritious fare, to the water tank where he enjoys nothing so much as a dip. Walter simply follows his feet along the textured edges of stone to get to where he wants to go. Of course, Mafalda continues to watch over him when he wanders off the path into the fresh, long grasses for a summer nap in his now and forever home.

11.9 Mafalda watching Walter in the pool; note the stone path

Chapter 12

❧ ❧ ❧ ❧ ❧ ❧ ❧ ❧ ❧ ❧ ❧ ❧ ❧ ❧ ❧ ❧
❧ ❧ ❧ ❧ ❧ ❧ ❧ ❧ ❧ ❧ ❧ ❧ ❧ ❧ ❧ ❧

Caring for Carnivores

We are driving to the Sanctuary on a pleasant Sunday morning in November to meet with Becca Miceli, Chief Science and Welfare Officer and Director of Animal Care. We often see Becca popping in and out of the Carnivore Nutrition Center (CNC) during our animal care shifts there. We have had a few quick conversations, but this is the first time we will be spending any amount of time with her. We are hoping she will give us a tour of the property, talk about her work here, and share her perspective on the animals under her care. In preparation, we reread newsletters. We review Becca's bio on the Sanctuary website. We prepare questions.

We also practice our chuffing – just in case. Tigers are quite vocal, and a "chuff" is among the sounds a tiger makes when it is happy. It sounds like a cross between a soft snuffle and a few gentle coughs; it is made by exhaling through the nose with the mouth closed, somewhat akin to a nicker from a contented horse. Tigers chuff when greeting and connecting with each other, and at the Sanctuary, with their caregivers and friends. As Kent Drotar observed when we heard more than a few chuffs directed his way during a visit to the Tiger Roundhouse, "I always say to people, if a tiger chuffs at you, it's rude not to chuff back." We hope not to insult any tigers, so we practice chuffing. It does not come naturally to us.

Becca has been with the Sanctuary for over two decades and has worked as a volunteer and staff member in so many different jobs and on so many different projects, they are beyond counting. Of her introduction to the Sanctuary, she tells us, "A lot of it was timing. I was at the right place at the right time. I was a tenacious eighteen year old knocking on Pat's door asking, 'Do you need help? I'll work for free!' I was always asking him questions, open to opportunities, and learning and engrossing myself in everything I could." Today, Becca is responsible for the health and wellness of the more than five hundred animals across three dozen species at the Sanctuary and the Refuge. She oversees a full time staff of eight animal caregivers, four animal medication specialists, and those who work at the CNC and in related areas. Becca also works closely with Sanctuary veterinarians to prep animals and oversee clinical procedures and surgeries, and then to manage post-operative care – perhaps one of the least appreciated but most confounding aspects of exotic animal surgeries. She is a veterinary technician and has completed coursework in nonprofit management, not to mention her previously-mentioned structural welding school stint more than a decade ago. During a two-year hiatus from the Sanctuary Becca worked in radiation oncology and critical care veterinary practices in California and Washington. Pat Craig describes Becca as "by far, the most experienced large carnivore medical technician in the country."

We spend a delightful morning. Zipping around the vast grounds in a four-wheeler, Becca talks to us about her job and her thoughts on exotic animal sentience and intelligence. She calls by name many of the animals we pass and answers questions on her walkie-talkie from animal caregivers who are on rounds and need to discuss one of their charges. Becca prefers the term "caregiver" to "caretaker" or to "animal keeper," explaining, "Keeper is the norm in the industry, but to me it's important to understand that we are here to 'give' something back that has been taken away." We visit the Tiger Roundhouse and make a trifling attempt at chuffing, trying not to embarrass ourselves in the process.

Becca later parks next to a habitat with some of the "Spain" lions rescued from Barcelona and lays out the hierarchy, "Melena Negra is the king in that pride, but Bruno is trying to take over...So the caregivers give Melana Negra his food first, then Bruno his food second, and then Bartolo gets his third." Makeisha (Mak) Ledbetter, one of the Sanctuary's four caregivers who administer medications, drives up and parks her four-wheeler next to the fence. "She is driving," Becca relates, "a special 'treat wagon.'"

In many zoos, clicker training, verbal cues, special treats, and other forms of operant conditioning enable zookeepers to move animals around and entice them toward keepers and veterinarians without frightening them. Dr. Felicia Knightly, senior veterinarian at the Memphis Zoo and Aquarium who consults regularly with the Sanctuary, has described to us the methods zoos employ to prompt chimps to turn a shoulder for an injection or harken a tiger to a fence so blood can be drawn from its tail. The large habitats at the Sanctuary are not conducive to operant conditioning methods, nor are such methods appropriate to its mission empowering wild animals to live as natural a life as possible. The "treat wagons" are, however, a form of positive reinforcement – kind of like "the ice cream truck in your neighborhood," laughs Dr. Joyce Thompson, the Sanctuary's full time veterinarian. "The treat wagon," says Becca, "always brings good things, so when it drives over to the fence the animals come running over. No lion would come over because you are calling them. They would be like 'oh, that's cute.' But when they see this vehicle, they are like, 'Yes! It is the chicken wagon!'"

Sure enough, Mak pulls a raw chicken breast out of a yellow bin and tucks pills into the meat for Flora, a lioness who requires daily pain medications for a patella problem. "We rotate the food all the time. So today Mak might have chicken, tomorrow she might have a red meat roast, the next day she might have chicken dunked in evaporated milk. That's the creativity of the med staff." Flora, it seems, can be a bit obstinate. Becca smiles, "One of Flora's biggest joys in life is being difficult for the meds staff…she watches them have breakdowns because they can't get her to take her meds." But Mak and Flora appear to have developed a mutual understanding about prescription chicken. Flora approaches the fence and Mak carefully pushes the skewered chicken through the steel grid. Mak watches Flora carefully. Mission accomplished, meds down the hatch! Mak hurries off to see her next patient and we drive off to see more lions and tigers.

Over the next few months, we will see Becca climb onto an operating table to listen to the heart and lungs of an anesthetized mountain lion, step out of a four-wheeler to heave a chicken quarter over the fence to tiger Diego, and have a lively conversation with Momo the camel. But right now, watching Mak tend to lioness Flora, who was ill-treated for so many years in Barcelona, and listening to Becca affectionately reel off one story after another about the quirks and foibles of dozens of the animals who live here, we have a greater appreciation for everyone at the Sanctuary who not only understands what it means to "give" back, but embodies the meaning of "care" in "caregiver." We also feel a tremendous pride for the backbreaking and messy work staff and volunteers do at the CNC.

The Daily Grind

Mark flips the toggle switch and the electric drive raises and tilts a barrel weighing somewhere around 250 pounds toward the edge of the stainless steel table. A cascade of mostly raw meat and poultry, hot dogs and salami, shrimp, and salmon slams onto the surface. We begin sorting through it. Packages are sliced open and plastic and Styrofoam tossed in the trash barrel. Most of the raw meat is destined for the industrial-size meat grinder and ultimately the big cats, but sausage and any raw meat that has been marinated, cured, or heavily spiced is flung into the trash because the big cats cannot metabolize spices. Chicken and turkey are tossed in the poultry barrel. Boneless beef is pitched into the red meat barrel once we have sliced out and jettisoned the bones. The same goes for pork. Debone the chop and fling the meat into the pork container. We heave large bone-in roasts and hams ("no smaller than a football" per the printed instructions overhead) into a fourth bin, boneless roasts into another, and whole raw chickens – after we have thrust our gloved hands into the cavity and pulled out any paper-wrapped giblets – into yet another.

Almost everything else goes into "bear barrels." Cooked sausage, hotdogs, cooked and raw shrimp, whole tilapia, a great slab of salmon, rotisserie chickens, lunch meat, doughnuts, and other assorted delicacies will delight the bears. "They're omnivores," says Leigh Mihlbauer, one of the CNC staff, "they will eat anything." When the first barrel winched onto the table has been apportioned, Mark retrieves another full of packaged meat and we begin again. The third barrel is full of apples, jalapenos, carrots, and other bear delicacies. Then another with loose meat and fish. And another. And another. And that is just the sorting operation.

The atmosphere at the CNC is casual but serious-minded. It is a beehive of activity every day of the year, hot in the summer and cold in the winter. "One thing about the CNC experience," volunteer Nancy Steffen has remarked, "is that you gain a real appreciation for how hard the staff works, the kind of dedication they have. Because they are doing that all the time, every day, no matter the weather. It knocks me out." Staff and volunteers wearing Sanctuary orange, waterproof boots, aprons, and all manner of gloves move quickly back and forth from the receiving dock to the preliminary refrigeration bay, to the sorting tables, to the flash freezer, and to the washup area where everything is hosed down and disinfected. Barrels with every food imaginable are hauled back and forth. The radio blasts. Trucks come and go. Animal caregivers rumble in and out in vans and four-wheelers to pick up buckets and barrels of food for their charges. The Wolfhounds occasionally swing by to see if a steak might be coming their way.

The work is hard; by the end of the shift your feet are tired and knees and back are aching. As volunteer Grant Steffen has observed about a day's work at the CNC, "I've found that standing a long time is more fatiguing than if I were to go out with some of the workers and pull weeds for an hour. But," he says brightly, "it's fine!" He is right. The job is dirty, slimy, sometimes smelly, and not recommended for anyone who cannot cope with a lot of raw meat – and we mean a lot of raw meat. The Sanctuary feeds more than 35,000 pounds of meat to the big cats and other carnivores and 37,000 pounds of additional assorted food to the bears – *each and every week.*

So, where does all the food come from?

For years, the Sanctuary purchased food for its residents; now the food comes mostly from about sixty grocers. Three refrigerated Sanctuary trucks wend their way among Front Range cities and towns collecting discarded food that is donated to the Sanctuary. The food donation process is made possible by the 1996 Bill Emerson Good Samaritan Food Donation Act (named after the late Congressman who was instrumental in its advancement) that removed liability from gleaners. The USDA defines gleaning as "the act of collecting excess fresh foods from farms, gardens, farmers markets, grocers, restaurants, state/county fairs, or any other sources in order to provide it to those in need." Although it took a while after the law was passed for gleaning systems to be put in place, charitable organizations, churches, and others acting in good faith by gathering and distributing food to the needy and hungry were now protected by law. Today, rather than being thrown away, unsold food is donated to homeless shelters, soup kitchens, and other organizations serving the hungry – and once those organizations have as much as they can use, to animal sanctuaries and shelters. The colloquial term for the process is, aptly, "food rescue." So the food that is rescued comes to the animals that were rescued and need to be fed. Perfect.

The food processing operation at the Sanctuary is designed to ensure that its residents get all the nutrients they require for healthy and vital lives. After the meat and produce has been sorted in separate barrels as described above, the process for big cats and other carnivores diverges from that for bears, reflecting the eating habits and dietary requirements of each.

The big cats, wolves, and other meat-eaters at the Sanctuary are fed a carefully formulated ground meat mixture, honed by forty years of experience in the carnivore kitchen. It may seem relatively straightforward to feed African lions, jaguars, leopards, and tigers. Just throw in a hunk of raw meat, right? No, it is not quite that easy. Take lions, for example. Yes, wild lions subsist primarily on red meat from prey such as antelopes, zebras, wild hogs, wildebeest, and other smaller mammals. But in doing so, they also consume a variety of nutrients that are not available in just muscle meat. For starters, lions pretty much eat the whole animal – not only the meat but bones, viscera, fatty tissue, and skin. Doing so provides them protein from the meat, calcium from bones, and vitamins A, D, E found in organs and fatty tissues. Big cats need these nutrients to stay healthy and all manner of diseases and disorders can arise if they are missing from their diets.

Young African lions with Vitamin A deficiencies, for example, are susceptible to fatal neurological disorders that occur because the skull growth plates fuse together before the young animals have finished growing. Insufficient calcium stores result in Metabolic Bone Disease (MBD) in big cats; we have seen the example of Pat's first young lion cub Leo, whose soft bones began to strengthen after Pat put him on a calcium-rich diet. Many animals arrive at the Sanctuary having been malnourished for a good portion of their lives; feeding a nutritionally-balanced diet often goes a long way toward the healing process.

So, for the big cats and other carnivores, once the food is sorted, a staff member fills the meat grinder with mostly beef and a smaller amount of poultry, and tops it off with a layer of pork, eggs and the sort of vitamin and mineral supplements that their wild brethren ingest from fresh kills. All are processed to a coarse grind, which is scooped and punched into metal buckets. The buckets are flash frozen. Frozen meat stays fresh longer and cleans the teeth of the meat-eaters. When it is time to feed, roughly four-inch thick by twelve-inch diameter frozen disks – resembling super thick, blood red Frisbees – are popped out of the buckets ready for distribution by the animal caregivers.

Bears forage for food, snuffling through the smorgasbord placed on the ground in their habitats until they find what suits them on any given day. Rotisserie chicken. Fried chicken. Lunchmeat. Hot dogs. Tuna. Shrimp. Scallops. Peaches. Apples. Grapes. Berries. Salad. Carrots. Celery. Jalapenos. Sandwiches. Glazed doughnuts. Marshmallows (a special favorite). And on and on. It is not uncommon to see a black bear strolling toward its den with a whole watermelon in his enormous jaws. There he or she will sit on the front porch, in a manner of speaking, and enjoy their snack while taking in the goings on in the neighborhood.

There is something so rewarding about working in the CNC. As volunteer Cynthia Streed puts it, "When you do animal care, it is personal, human, compassionate. You get the whole picture; how important it is

12.1 Becca readies the bear buffet

to you and the animals. It is how I feel about this place, and how this place makes me feel. How it's healed me." As dirty and exhausting as the work can be, staff and volunteers know they are taking care of the animals firsthand, laboring like butchers-in-training so that their four-legged friends can eat healthy food. Plus, sometimes volunteers get to help deliver the daily meal.

Mark is feeding big cats and wolves with Mackenzie Rolles on a sunny and frigid afternoon in January. First, they transfer heavy, slippery, frozen beef roasts from the bin on the dock to a fresh barrel. Then they muscle another half dozen barrels, each holding hundreds of pounds of frozen ground meat disks, along the dock and onto the back of an open bed truck. When the truck is loaded, Mackenzie hops behind the wheel, Mark takes the passenger seat and off they go for lions, tigers, and wolves. Stopping first at the habitat housing African lions Cana, Dian, Leo and Leon, Mackenzie and Mark fling the frozen roasts over the fence. The entire pride pounds toward them, not only the males but females Gala, Zinna, and Zoya, stopping just on the other side of the fence. Cana pounces on one of the roasts as it thuds on the frozen ground. He takes his prize across the field and lays down with a satisfied thump. Sol and Luna next door have caught sight of the food truck and are making their way briskly across the field. Sol also stops next to the fence. It is a heady experience to be this close to a five hundred pound African lion. As volunteer Joe Spahn relates, "With Animal Care you spend a whole lot of time doing tedious stuff for the opportunity to go out and help feed the animals. That's the closest you get to them...They are looking at you and interacting with you and you are talking to them." But right now there's little opportunity to get caught up in the thrill of the moment; that will come later when Mark can relish the fact that he just spent two hours feeding some of the greatest creatures on the planet. Now it is time to move on and Mackenzie and Mark work rapidly as a team to deliver the evening meals. At each habitat, Mark helps unload and Mackenzie flings frozen meat Frisbees over the fences; both stuff freezing fingers into jacket pockets and jump into the warmth of the truck cab to speed off to the next hungry horde. It is a job that is repeated in more than eighty habitats for more than 500 animals by a handful of animal caregivers and their volunteer helpers, day in and day out.

12.2 Lions enjoying "meat disks" for dinner

Celebrating One and All

Over the course of the eighteen months in which we researched and wrote this book and volunteered in Animal Care and Education, we came to a profound appreciation of the Sanctuary's most elemental credo: no matter how many animals live at the Sanctuary, each of them is an individual with their own distinct needs and preferences and desires. They are not just lions or tigers or grizzly bears or lynx or wolves. They are not just orthopedic problems, or vision problems, or the aches associated with aging. They are not a diagnosis waiting to happen, or a salve for our egos, or an exotic animal exhibited for our entertainment. They are as original, unique, and idiosyncratic as every single one of us.

Not long ago while sorting meat in the CNC, we watched longtime animal caregiver Eric Bruner carefully carve away two boneless chicken breasts from a whole bird, while standing next to a 32-gallon bin brimming with boneless chicken breasts. If he needed boneless chicken breasts, we asked, why not just grab a few from the bin? He was making the extra effort, he explained, because a lioness named Guera preferred chicken breasts fresh off the bone to those packaged in Styrofoam and plastic wrap. His "very special lady" had very discerning tastes, and her acutely sensitive taste buds preferred the more unprocessed, natural flavor of the genuine article rather than meat tainted by the flavors of artificial packing materials. She was not just another lioness, she was Guera. Becca sums it up:

> My biggest role is managing the overall wellness of the animals at the Sanctuary. Are they treated as individuals? Are they getting what they need? Because they are all different. You can look at one lion and he might need somebody who is just going to give him a chicken every day and drive on. Or you might have another lion who needs you to sit there for five minutes acknowledging that he is there, acknowledging his existence, fussing over him, and then moving on."

Every single animal at the Sanctuary has a unique personality. Clay, Daniel, Enzo, and Thomas, the four Oklahoma tigers who moved to the "tiger temple" habitat, "are a great group of four young tigers who just enjoy each other's company," Becca tells us, "They play, they roughhouse, but they are all very respectful of each other." As evidenced by this photo of Clay lounging atop the tiger temple, they also clearly like to climb!

Milo, another giant of a tiger, loves to throw a three-foot long, twelve-inch diameter log into his freshwater tank and then splash in after it. He pulls it out, rolls it around in the dirt, and flings it back in again and again. The animal caregivers shake their heads, resigned to the fact that they must change Milo's water more often than that of his tiger neighbors.

12.3 Clay atop the tiger temple, enjoying...

12.4 another routine day in paradise

Trouble, a thousand-pound grizzly, is characterized by Kent Drotar as a "pretty nervous bear." African lion Baby Leo thrives on attention but not too much; he is just learning how to lead a pride and too much hanging out with humans would be unseemly. White tiger Timara's ears vibrate when she chuffs. Jumanji, the black leopard, is in love with Becca who, of course, speaks "leopard" so she and "Manj," as he is affectionately known, greet each other daily in typical big cat fashion – approach slowly from the side, bow your head, lower your gaze, and press your forehead gently against your friend's forehead through the steel fence. Natasha, a grizzly bear who lives with Boris and Tiny, is renowned for her swiftness in chasing the food truck that races along the road outside her habitat's perimeter fence. Anyone lucky enough to witness Natasha's speed walks away with a renewed grasp for why savvy hikers do their best to avoid grizzly bears in the wild.

Years ago, an African lion named Shane needed a hemilaminectomy, a type of back surgery to address his inflamed spinal cord. His post-op care required that Becca return to the Sanctuary every evening around 10:00 p.m. to administer IV and physical therapy on the massive, immobilized cat. During his treatments she would put her iPhone music on shuffle. "Bastille would come on" she recalls, "and Shane would be very calm. We would be doing passive range of motion…He would close his eyes and I would massage his back. Then Eminem would come on and he would growl and open his eyes and look at me. So I would fast forward. I would tell Pat, 'this lion does not like Eminem.'" Shane, it seems, could pick out Eminem regardless of the song and the shuffle sequence; Becca, quite sensibly, would quickly find another more agreeable tune.

Consider these anecdotes in light of Joe Exotic's comment to Becca when the Sanctuary team was at his Wynnewood zoo to rescue thirty-nine tigers and four bears. Becca asked Joe, "Can you tell me anything about them?" Joe turned to her and said, "After you have 120 tigers, their names and personalities don't matter anymore."

Sorry Joe, but once again you got it wrong.

By contrast, staff and volunteers at the Sanctuary celebrate the singularity of each and every animal, treating all with respect, concern, and love. For those who would call white tigers enchanted or royal or mystical, we would counter that they *are* extraordinarily special – but not because of their white coats. Diego is special not because he is a white tiger but because he is Diego! Giant Kodiak bear Max was not special because he was one of the largest, fiercest land mammals in the world but because he was Max! Bob and Percy are not special because they were among the last African lions out of Bolivia when the circuses closed but because they are Bob and Percy! Like all the animals who call the Sanctuary home, they are special not because of *what* they are but because of *who* they are.

At The Wild Animal Sanctuary, every animal matters and caring for them may be among the most altruistic of vocations. Becca tells the animal care staff, "These are wild animals and you'll do great here if you don't need them to love you back…We should give to all the animals everything they need to make their lives better as individuals." Becca fully appreciates and impresses upon the animal caregivers the reality that "it's okay for them not to need us, not to depend on us, to just be allowed to be whoever they are." A sense of giving back, a commitment to easing suffering, to making a difference for at least one animal is what motivated Pat to begin rescuing large carnivores more than forty years ago. It also is what animates the enthusiasm and initiative among staff and volunteers, one of the most visible manifestations of the work ethic that powers The Wild Animal Sanctuary today.

Chapter 13

🐾 🐾 🐾 🐾 🐾 🐾 🐾 🐾 🐾 🐾 🐾 🐾 🐾 🐾 🐾 🐾

The Doctor – and Dentist – Are In

R onin, a big, blond, handsome African lion with a full, shaggy mane and massive face is staring at us from a few feet away. He occasionally shakes his head and utters a low growl. It is thrilling to be this close to an African lion in his prime – almost four feet at the shoulder and at least 400 pounds – and we are thankful there is a high-tensile game fence between us. Ronin exudes the power, self-confidence, and potency of the apex predator of the African savannah. He also is sporting a dollop of Reddi-wip whipped cream on his nose. Somehow, it does not detract from his majestic and regal demeanor.

We are doing rounds with Becca Miceli and Dr. Felicia Knightly, who flew in from Memphis for the weekend. Felicia began visiting the Sanctuary and then providing veterinary services for the animals while working as a veterinarian at the Denver Zoo. With almost three decades of exotic animal experience, she has traveled the world conducting fieldwork, operating on, anaesthetizing, and caring for animals. She became the senior veterinarian at the Memphis Zoo and Aquarium in 2011 but continues to travel to Denver to consult with and perform surgeries at the Sanctuary. The Sanctuary's on-site full time veterinarian, Dr. Joyce Thompson is not on the property today; we will catch up with her later.

Becca has a whole line up of animals for Felicia to see today; Ronin and his lioness companion Zephyr are numbers two and three on the list. We start the day off with Morrison, aka Momo, a tall Dromedary camel who came to the Sanctuary in 2005 from an Erie, Colorado horse boarding facility that was closing its doors. Momo appears to have a swelling of some sort on the inside of his left front foot. Becca jerks the four-wheeler into park and approaches the perimeter fence, calling out in a clear, ringing voice, "Momo!" About fifty feet away, the great humped Dromedary turns his head and fixes his heavily lidded gaze

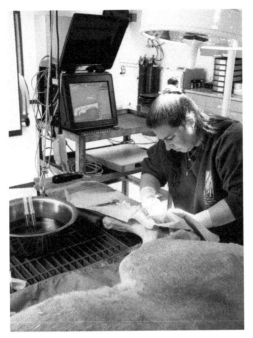
13.1 Dr. Felicia Knightly at the Sanctuary Clinic

upon us. "Momo!" Becca calls again. Momo lifts a foreleg and then slowly, slowly, and deliberately glides across the paddock toward us. Camels can run forty miles an hour; Momo is clearly in first gear. We chat amongst ourselves as we wait for this "great ship of the desert" to dock. When Momo finally reaches the fence, he lowers his head and solemnly regards Becca through his double-thick long lashes. She strokes his nose, chattering away, feeding him Keebler Graham Crackers, and offering him a bit of Mountain Dew. He happily slurps it up. We must clarify, at this point, that Keebler Graham Crackers, Mountain Dew, and other similar treats are *not* standard fare on Sanctuary residents' menus. However, think about the lollipops and party favors that are mainstays at the pediatrician's office, not to mention jars of dog and cat treats at the veterinarian's office. Sometimes a "spoonful of sugar" – or graham crackers or Mountain Dew – are just what the doctor ordered.

In any case, Momo enjoys his special treat and Becca and Felicia spend a good half hour considering a variety of causes for his slightly misshapen ankle. When both are satisfied that they have covered the possibilities and developed a plan of action, everyone piles back into the vehicle and off we go.

13.2 Momo enjoying his Mountain Dew

When we first arrive at the Lion House, Zephyr is inside but Ronin is lounging on the outside "patio." Becca pushes raw chicken pieces through the fence; Zephyr crunches the bones like they are a handful of potato chips. She has been suffering from a persistent limp on her left front leg since she and Ronin were rescued about six months ago. Becca and Felicia quietly discuss her injury. Is it her shoulder? Elbow? Ankle? Paw? Is her leg turning out? Has the lameness gotten worse? Has there been a loss of muscle mass? How does the left leg compare to the right leg? They study her gait as she moves around the enclosure. Felicia takes photos with her smartphone. During the discussion, Becca intermittently calls out, "Ronin!" After about twenty minutes Becca and Felicia wrap up their ruminations on Zephyr's lameness, and as we swallow our disappointment about not seeing Ronin today, he suddenly appears in the small doorway. His enormous head and mane fill the opening and he trots briskly inside, striding boldly to the fence where he too is rewarded with raw chicken. Ronin has a few small polyps on his face and on his legs; another ten minutes pass as the two discuss these barely visible tiny bumps. More pondering. More pictures. Felicia questions whether he has any of the growths inside his mouth.

Becca reaches into the back of the vehicle for the secret weapon in the culinary toolkit of exotic animal veterinarians and keepers – Reddi-wip whipped cream. Becca squeezes the whipped cream into Ronin's mouth through the steel grid of the fence and he runs his tongue around his mouth and over his nose. She squeezes and he laps. Soon whipped cream coats the big cat's whiskery face, dribbles down the fence, glazes his toes, and puddles on the straw below. After about twenty minutes and most of the contents of a can of Reddi-wip, Becca and Felicia conclude their examination and discussion. An hour has passed since we arrived at the Lion House. The Reddi-wip is tucked amid the other trappings of large carnivore care and then it is on to the next patient. Ronin is still licking the leftovers around his mouth as Becca drives away.

So many of the animals who are rescued by the Sanctuary need medical attention. Some suffer greatly from years of having lived a hard life. Some arrive so gaunt and emaciated it is a wonder they are still alive; others are morbidly obese from too much junk food and too-small cages. Many are simply old and beset by the same sort of geriatric afflictions that affect us all – arthritis, disc compression, cataracts, renal problems, and cancer, among them. The Sanctuary has an on-site clinic specially equipped for handling exotic animals ranging from the smallest coati mundi to the greatest of bears and tallest of camels. Most procedures are performed at the Sanctuary; when more sophisticated diagnostics and complex surgeries are needed the animal is taken to the highly regarded College of Veterinary Medicine at Colorado State University in Fort Collins, a little over an hour away.

Commonplace, But Never Routine

There is nothing routine about clinical procedures for wild animals because all require sedation, which is used sparingly because it can be risky. For humans, and pet dogs and cats, pre-operative protocols include blood work and physical exams to alert doctors to underlying medical conditions. It is impossible to do such screening for many exotic animals. So, if an animal is going to be sedated, the watchword is, as Felicia quips, "Make the most out of the immobilization." When an animal needs to undergo one of the more commonplace procedures at the Clinic, such as sterilization, the relief of chronic problems resulting from declawed feet, or dental procedures, the medical team uses the necessary sedation to take care of as many other tasks as possible, including benchmark wellness exams. While the doctors are working at one end (or the other) the Sanctuary medical team draws blood, takes the animal's temperature, palpates its abdomen, checks paws, trims nails, examines limbs, and records heart rate and other vital signs.

A true sanctuary never breeds its residents, so one of the Sanctuary's top priorities is to prevent all reproduction. Every male animal rescued is neutered except male lions, who lose their manes if neutered. Instead, the female lions are given contraceptive implants. Unless the newly rescued animal is too unhealthy to cope with the surgery, the sterilization is scheduled within a few days of arrival.

Although neutering is typically done by the Sanctuary's veterinarians, Dr. Jeff Young of Animal Planet's hit show, *Dr. Jeff: Rocky Mountain Vet*, has also pitched in from time to time with sterilizations, dental work, claw trimming and more. Dr. Jeff is famous for his Planned Pethood Plus clinic in Wheat Ridge, Colorado, and his advocacy for spaying and neutering pets. Since his primary focus in that department has been on dogs and cats, he has welcomed the opportunity to treat bigger felids and has donated his time to the Sanctuary over the years.

Cucho, a tiger who was rescued from a private owner in Pachuca, Mexico was neutered on Dr. Jeff's Animal Planet show in June 2019. It is a miracle that Cucho, who suffered a severe back injury before coming to the Sanctuary, can even walk. Yet, like so many rescued animals, he has an indomitable spirit. Sedating is especially tricky for Cucho since the medical team must take extreme care in moving him. The Sanctuary team had thought that Cucho would live alone in the Tiger Roundhouse because of his mobility issues but when it became clear that he and next

13.3 Simba and Cucho

door neighbor Simba (yes, Simba is a female tiger; the original owner was apparently confused about the fact that the word means "lion" in Swahili) were becoming good friends, the Sanctuary team decided to make them roommates. About a month after Cucho was neutered, he and Simba were introduced in a grassy transitional habitat and have been living together ever since.

Many of the large carnivores rescued by the Sanctuary have been declawed, a deceptively benign name for an appalling surgery akin to amputating a person's finger through the joint above the fingernail. Big cats, smaller cats like lynx and bobcats, and bears are routinely declawed by owners in futile attempts to render wild animals less dangerous. Not only is declawing itself inhumane but the aftereffects – podiatric problems, limping, infections, and skeletal issues – are exceedingly painful and require what would otherwise be unnecessary medical procedures. "Don't even get me started on declawing," vows Felicia, "Think about it. You are a cub and someone declawed you with bolt cutters in their garage. Because you were twenty-five pounds then and you're now 350 pounds and all the ligaments and all the muscles and every joint that goes from the declawed foot all the way up the limb have been affected by how you have compensated throughout your life. It is heartbreaking." Many declawed animals, Cucho included, suffer from an excruciating condition where their claws continually grow back but are deformed and pierce the pads of the feet causing lameness and ongoing infections. The animals must be sedated so the medical staff can trim, disengage, and disinfect the claw beds.

Then there are the toothaches. About fifty percent of rescues arrive at the Sanctuary in agony from chronic tooth infections caused by having their teeth pulled or filed down in another failed effort to make the animals safer for humans. The irony is that while owners of exotic animals go to extremes to protect themselves, they provide almost no basic veterinary care for the animals – and dental neglect is one of the worst. Mouth problems arise not only from inhumane measures but from poor nutrition, gum disease, stress-induced cage biting, and an overall lack of veterinary care.

Is there anyone out there who has not had a toothache? Just the thought of an aching cavity, an infected incisor, or an excruciating abscess is enough to make most of us moan in anguish. A tiger has thirty teeth, with upper canines 2.5 to 3 inches long, and a bear has forty-two teeth – in both cases, a lot of teeth with which to suffer dental problems. Can you imagine being a 1,000-pound grizzly bear or 500-pound lion with a chronic toothache and no way to tell anyone about it? Felicia observes, "These animals can be amazingly stoic. It is part of being a wild animal because if they show weakness they are at risk...but if you had the kind of arthritis or the kind of neuromuscular disease or the kind of dental disease that some of these animals have had, you would be curled up in a ball in the corner...Their pain tolerance is something people cannot understand." Unfortunately, many of the Sanctuary's rescues require serious dental procedures.

The Peter Emily International Veterinary Dental Foundation (PEIVDF) established in Lakewood, Colorado in 2005, has been a lifeline for suffering exotic animals not only at the Sanctuary but around the world. Peter Emily, DDS, has been a pioneer in exotic animal dentistry since performing root canal therapy on a tiger in the 1970s. The Foundation has performed close to 700 root canal therapies and more than 500 extractions on hundreds of animals ranging from lions, tigers, and bears to elephants, rhinoceros, and hippos (not to mention a penguin with a beak alignment problem). It has become one of the most important educators, promoters, and purveyors of captive wildlife dental health in the world. Dr. Emily has been a tireless

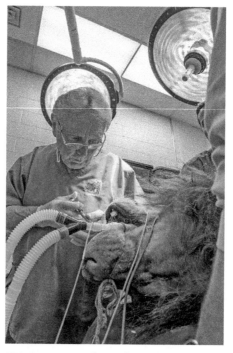

13.4 Dr. Peter Emily working on Güero,
an African lion

defender of the need for exotic animal oral and dental healthcare arguing that "every animal has to do two things to survive. Number one, they have to move. Number two, they have to eat." Without the locomotion to get to the food the animal will not likely survive, but if it is unable to eat the food, it will surely die.

With its location about forty-five miles from Keenesburg, PEIVDF has undertaken more missions to The Wild Animal Sanctuary than anywhere else. Remember Colo Colo, the angry African lion rescued from Bolivia in 2011? Colo Colo's whole attitude changed after Dr. Emily performed root canal therapy on his broken and infected canine tooth. White tiger Diego suffered from an impacted molar and a fractured premolar. The first problem was likely a congenital condition arising from white tiger inbreeding; the second was likely caused by a blow to the face with a heavy object. Again Foundation dentists stepped in and Diego was relieved of years of pain.

Two of the most common large carnivore dental procedures at the Sanctuary are root canal therapies and tooth extractions (which may be among the most dreaded words in the English language). How, we wonder, do you perform root canal therapies or extract a tooth on a tiger, or a lion, or a bear? And who does large carnivore dental work? We are about to find out because Andromeda's mouth needs some serious attention and her dental appointment is scheduled for a Saturday in February.

Andromeda is a beautiful female African lion who is six years old. She was rescued in 2015, along with her sisters Miranda and Luna, from a Pachuca, Mexico zoo that was shuttered because it was unable to care for the animals. The three sisters live with Jupiter and his two sisters, Terra and Venus, all of whom were also rescued from the same zoo at the same time. Although Andromeda is quite young for such extensive dental work, her stress-driven "cage biting" and substandard care at the zoo has caught up with her.

Root canal therapy is used to stop a tooth infection so that a later tooth extraction can be avoided. Big cats need their teeth for tearing and chewing, so extractions are considered a last resort. Plus, as noted by Dr. Emily and Susanne Pilla, a founding member of PEIVDF, unless the tooth is already loose and wobbly, an extraction is like "trying to remove a raw egg from a block of cement." Andromeda needs root canal therapy on four teeth. A challenging procedure on any species, the length and depth of the roots of large carnivore teeth, traveling along the lower jaw to the back molars and along the upper jaw almost to the eyes, up the ante on difficulty.

Andromeda, who was sedated in the Lion House, is carefully lifted onto the operating table at the clinic. Joyce intubates the big lioness and starts the anesthesia. Joyce, Becca, and Ryan Clements immediately begin their examination. Afterward, Becca covers Andromeda with a heated blanket to keep her warm and comfortable.

13.5 Ryan, Joyce, and Becca examine Andromeda

The dentists draw her enormous head toward them and lift her upper jaw onto a curved and padded metal bar suspended on metal posts from the ceiling. Gently placing the metal "sling" just behind her upper canines, they allow her lower jaw to naturally sag into an open, and accessible, position. They cushion and support her lower jaw with a stack of folded towels.

13.6 Andromeda and two of her dentists, Dr. Hall and Dr. Dyer

Four dentists are on hand for Andromeda's surgery. Doctors Charlie Dyer and Brad LeValley are "people" dentists with a passion for animal care; Charlie hails from Texas and Brad from Fort Collins, Colorado. Dr. Barron Hall has flown in from Virginia where he is the owner of the Animal Dental Clinic and is a veterinary dentist at the National Zoo in Washington, D.C. Dr. Clarence Sitzman has been in veterinary dentistry for more than four decades and has long been associated with PEIVDF; his enthusiasm for the task at hand is apparent. He keeps calling us over to peer into Andromeda's mouth as he explains the procedure.

At one point three dentists are working in Andromeda's mouth at the same time. Susanne Pilla calls it "octopus dentistry." It is a practice made imperative by the need to minimize the sedation period for any large carnivore. Three or four sets of hands working on as many teeth simultaneously will get Andromeda off the operating table in a third or a fourth the time it would take one dentist working alone. Root canal therapy involves drilling a small hole either on the side or through the fractured crown of the tooth and removing the infected pulp from its center. Once the tooth has been fully cleaned out, the void is filled with a bioactive material, such as a form of calcium hydroxide, and then sealed using a dental composite and a curing light. Dexterous dentists' fingers and instruments fly in and out of Andromeda's mouth and in about two hours the tawny lioness is good to go. She can rejoin the pride and will not even have to suffer through several hours of slowly subsiding Lidocaine.

Big cats are not the only animals who arrive at the Sanctuary with dental problems. Bears often need root canal therapy and extractions. Dillan, the Asiatic black bear rescued from the sportsman's club in Pennsylvania, arrived with a tooth infection so bad it had eaten through the fleshy tissue of his mouth. "Dillan's mouth was a complete disaster," moans Pat. "It was absolutely ravaged by widespread infection and long-term decay." Fortunately, dentists at PEIVDF rearranged their schedules to help Dillan within a few days of his arrival at the Sanctuary.

Dentists removed two canine teeth and all the lower teeth along the front of Dillan's mouth and performed root canal therapy on his other two broken canines. Thankfully, Dillan's molars did not require extraction, and with the help of medications to get through the post-operative pain, Dillan was eating soft food and fruit juices the next morning.

Dillan's remarkable recovery was not unusual. The relief of chronic pain often engenders immediate positive changes in temperament, a scenario that plays out time and again at the Sanctuary. "There are cases where I can't even imagine the pain," Pat admits. But when the pain can be eliminated through prudent surgeries or managed through the appropriate pain medications, "You can see the physical change. They are bright and perky, and suddenly they want to do things..." Dillan is a case in point; within a couple of days his whole demeanor began to change, and he started organizing the toys in his introduction enclosure.

13.7 Andromeda

Beyond Commonplace Care

Although more than ninety percent of the animals rescued by the Sanctuary do not have major medical problems, a few arrive fighting for their lives. Some, despite the best efforts of Sanctuary and CSU doctors and medical staff, do not make it. Others do; Morelia, the lioness clubbed over the head in the Tarzan circus act; Fifi, the Syrian brown bear who languished behind bars for three decades; Jumanji, the black leopard from Ohio who suffered from uric acid burns and frostbite. Pat calls them "true survivors." These are the animals that have endured horrific conditions that would be the end of most of us. Not only have they been rescued from situations in which they were suffering, starving, and undergoing physical and psychological abuse, but after being rescued, many must then undergo medical tests, surgeries, physical therapy, and other similar procedures. This is where the miracles begin.

Marley is a "sweet and gentle female grizzly bear" who was rescued by the Sanctuary in 2014. She arrived limping on one front leg. The limp worsened, as did the noticeable hunch in her back, which appeared to be compensation for the pain. The medical team drove Marley to CSU where it was discovered that she had not just one broken front leg, but two! Both had been broken in the same place recently, just below the elbow! Coincidence? Accident? Intentional harm? We will never know, but the nature of the breaks suggested that a fall was unlikely.

Marley's front legs were already starting to mend, although not as perfectly as they would have if the previous owner had called a doctor immediately. So, why was she still limping so badly? Further examination found a bone fragment from the original break that had become lodged in the leg and infected; the veterinarians removed the fragment and began treatment of the infection with antibiotics.

After a successful surgery, Marley had to be monitored and kept calm in the Sanctuary's clinic for an extended period. The medical team kept her

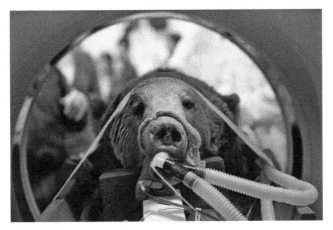

13.8 Marley at Colorado State University
Photo by John Eisele/Colorado State University Photography

busy: Marley watched cartoons and nature shows, learned to play hide-and-seek with the blankets on her bed, and spent hours working through a fire hose puzzle to retrieve the vegetables braided within. She has since served as a surrogate Mama Bear to Eva, an orphaned youngster who arrived at the Sanctuary and needed a friend.

13.9 Marley and her blankets back at the Sanctuary clinic

As Marley's story and so many others demonstrate, aside from the medical procedure itself and the risks of sedation associated with it, equally important and challenging is the management of post-operative care. In fact, required care and recovery time are always major considerations and potential obstacles to surgery. Felicia, Joyce, and Becca can recall situations where they have had to challenge the viability of a needed surgery simply because there was no way they were going to be able to keep the large carnivore immobile for weeks on end. Keeping a tiger or a bear under wraps for an extended period is a little more complicated than putting a "cone of shame" on your recently neutered Boxer or keeping your Bulldog on a leash to allow his surgically repaired ACL to fully heal. In many ways the true care begins after the surgery ends.

Where Patience *is* a Virtue

Our impressions from doing rounds with Becca and Felicia? Talking to Joyce about a never-typical day at the Sanctuary? Observing dental procedures on a young lioness named Andromeda? And digesting the medical miracles and comeback stories of the true survivors? One word: incredible! There are a lot of things that go into large carnivore and exotic animal medical care: keen powers of observation; the enormous value of technological changes that allow medical staff to detect and document medical conditions; and the patience required to discern and diagnose all manner of minor ailments and serious conditions.

We were struck by the observation skills of the medical team and caregivers. Joyce has described moving from a small animal medical practice to the Sanctuary. At the former she was able to literally feel her way to a diagnosis on dogs and cats; now she must visually assess more than 500 exotics from a distance. It was a major change in technique, she explained, in which "I had to go from touching to seeing." Medical staff and regular animal caregivers must be able to recognize what is normal for a given tiger or lion or fox or camel and watch for deviations from that normalcy. The only way to do that is to study the animal – how it eats, where it sleeps, how it moves, when it seems sad or simply uncomfortable. Since the medical team is unable to pry open a lion's mouth to peek at his three inch long canines, Joyce comments:

> What we look for are changes in the way they eat, the prehension and the mastication, the way they take the food into their mouth and the way they bite it and then the way they chew it and swallow. They may only want to chew out of one side of their mouth. They may be reluctant to eat certain things like bone-in chicken...Sometimes we will actually get an opportunity to see their teeth. They'll yawn or as they take hold of treats or food, we'll get a pretty good view of their mouth and most of their dentition.

Felicia explains how observation becomes a fixation, "People are in awe of watching animals cross the habitat. But I'm watching them walk and saying, 'he's got a subtle lameness of that left hind leg. I need to know why. Chronic? A little arthritis? Did he sprain or strain something? Did another animal 'cheap shot' him and he has a little wound? Does he have something as simple as a little overgrown nail?' There are all those things to take into consideration. It becomes an obsession."

Diagnostics are made easier through technology. MRIs, CAT scans, and other cutting-edge medical technologies provide a level of problem-solving acumen unavailable one or two decades ago. Even something as ordinary as a smart phone with a sophisticated camera can today record or relay instantaneous information that would have been impossible fifteen years ago. Medical procedures are undertaken cautiously. Anesthesia, a modern medical miracle but not without risks, is administered as infrequently as possible and used to establish markers for future use that would not otherwise be feasible.

Above all, we continue to be amazed and humbled by the steadfast patience of the medical team, and the deliberate pace and slow tenor of the diagnostic process. There is no hurrying Momo. Ronin will not come when called, he just comes along when he is ready. Zephyr will not hold up a paw so you can check between the pads. It is all part and parcel of wild animal medical care. Your patients do not speak English, so they cannot tell you how they feel. Many are enormous, in pain, stoic beyond belief, and highly dangerous. As rescues, most arrive here with little available information on their personal or medical histories. Post-operative care can be prohibitively problematic. And then there are the tough decisions related to age, mobility, and long term care. It is a challenge but mostly, says Joyce, "It is a privilege to work with this population because they are so deserving of good care. They've been through so much and being able to make their remaining days and years as good as they can be – that's pretty fabulous."

Because, as always, the animals at the Sanctuary are loved as the individuals that they are. If Shane prefers Bastille, so be it. Marley likes blankets, so here is a bundle. If Reddi-wip and Mountain Dew are the snacks of choice, bring them on. Becca explains with a grin, "There's a point in life where you are old enough or sick enough, that you can have whatever you want. I sure hope one day wherever I end up, if I do not want red Jell-O, someone goes and gets me orange Jell-O. Why wouldn't I do that same thing for each of them?" Regardless of where the residents of The Wild Animal Sanctuary are in their lives, whether tumbling toddlers or teetering oldsters, whether in good health or bad, they each receive all the empathy, protection, and sensitivity their caregivers can muster.

Chapter 14

Happy Days (and Wild Nights)
on the Walkway

On a scorching summer afternoon, a tiger strolls through the tall
summer grass, moving softly and deliberately toward the Walkway.
She lays down in the shade directly below us, completely oblivious to
the flurry of excitement she is creating among the visitors above. Facing
outward toward the grassy field, she keeps her head up, watching,
listening, completely relaxed. Visitors, especially the youngsters, are
thrilled. Everyone keeps their voices at a whisper. The crowd watches as
she angles her tufted ears back and forth and flicks her long tail gently
and slowly, marveling at the enormity of her paws. She never even glances
up toward us, a validation of Pat's insight almost forty years ago that
large carnivores are unfazed by activity well above them. After about
twenty minutes, she rises gracefully, pads slowly across the deep green
meadow, and then suddenly disappears. The only trace of this completely
unexpected gift is the elongated depression in the tall grass where the
tiger lay.

No matter the season, or the weather, there is magic on the Walkway.
We laugh at the antics of the grizzly bears and marvel at the tranquility of
a black leopard in repose on the sky bridge. We are awed by the majesty
of all the wild animals here. We are humbled by their wildness and
buoyed by their well-being. As volunteer Jim Anderson tells Sanctuary
visitors, "the animals won the lottery when they got here. No matter
how bad the situation was where they came from, even though they have
sad stories, this is the place where they come and live the rest of their
lives happily." We are witness every day to wild animal contentment and
companionship.

14.1 Grizzly bear yoga anyone?

Chumlee, one of five Syrian brown bears in a habitat near the Lion House, has been digging a shallow depression near his sizable swimming hole. He unhurriedly hollows out the ground, scraping dirt to one side for the better part of a half hour. Chumlee, it turns out, is gently crafting a bear "Barcalounger." Soon he settles his great bulk into the cavity, wriggling against the back of his newly fashioned chair until he is comfortable. Then he looks up and begins watching the visitors on the Walkway. We are watching Chumlee and Chumlee is watching us. He looks like he has settled in for the afternoon game and could not be more pleased with himself.

14.2 Chumlee in his bear "Barcalounger"

White tiger Diego has recently been moved from the Tiger Roundhouse to a luxurious habitat with trees for shade, boulders for lounging, and a deluxe kidney-shaped pool for swimming. On a stunning autumn afternoon, Diego is lounging on his favorite boulder. Quietly taking in the activity around him, he gazes calmly toward his tiger neighbors, catches a glimpse of Tiny the grizzly bear as he lumbers across the meadow next door, glances up at the visitors on the Walkway, and then quickly averts his head as a four-wheeler zips around the corner. Might it be Becca with a chicken treat? Not this time; the vehicle moves on and so does the massive white cat. Diego rises, stretches, drops gently to the ground, and silently glides into his den for a nap.

14.3 Diego takes a bow

On a frigid October afternoon, the wind is brisk, and the mountains have disappeared behind a cloud cover that continues to thicken and lower. The enormous Welcome Center, clearly visible through the open door of the Lion House, vanishes in a fog of mist and sleet. The Walkway glistens with ice. We are working a shift with volunteers Joe Spahn and Dee Pierce. There are few animals out and about and even fewer visitors. We see no leopards or jaguars. We greet a half dozen visitors who are bundled up, and on their way out of the Sanctuary. Lion Jupiter and a few lionesses are lounging in the winter-killed grass. Baby lynx Chester and his mother are ensconced in one of the pet igloos in their enclosure, paws and noses pointing out; heads lifted to catch the scent on the wind, ears tilting this way and that.

Without warning, the lions start roaring. Ronin and Orion get things going in the Lion House. Temuco, two doors down, picks up the cry and soon, he, Lambert, Bob, Percy, Nancy, and then more and more lions are all in on the tumult! Even Sampson, Tabitha, and Lacey, who live a half mile away near the Lion Deck, join in. The African lion's roar is the loudest and strongest of the big cats. A full-bodied roar can hit 114 decibels, comparable to music at a rock concert, and can be heard five miles away. The lions

14.4 Lions under the Walkway in winter

seem to be staging their own rock concert because the Lion House echoes with mighty, thunderous roars. Just when we think it cannot get any more intense, the pandemonium dies off as quickly as it started.

On a winter morning, we catch something in our peripheral vision. A large brown blur speeds by, about ten feet in front and above us, moving fast and flying west. A bald eagle! His white head and tail gleam in the morning sun. He swings to the south and alights on a nearby habitat fence post. Folding his wings he gazes sharply south. We have never seen an eagle this close before! What an unforgettable experience!

By noon, we have seen at least forty bald eagles.

They swoop in from all directions. They soar and dip, a flash of instantly recognizable white, brilliant against the topaz sky. Mottled youngsters, not yet sporting their signature white mantle, follow the leaders. Commandeering fence posts and tree branches laid bare by winter; they perch. Then they wait. And they watch. Jupiter's pride of African lions is working its way through a recently delivered sumptuous meal of meat disks and red roasts. When the big cats have had their fill and slowly move away from the feast, two dozen eagles dive toward the remains. They dance along patches of hard-packed snow to grab morsels of red meat. Then, with a single stroke of their massive wings, each is airborne seeking the high ground – in this case telephone poles – to tear into its share of the bounty. Pat Craig calls it "Nature's Cafeteria."

The eagles do not dine alone. Starlings, falcons, hawks, and similarly opportunistic predators enjoy the bounty of the Sanctuary's feasts. During the summer, seagulls, practiced at following farmers' plows as they turn the soil to expose buried nutrients and sumptuous earthworms, avail themselves of the fruits and seeds left at the bear buffets. The mutually agreeable Sanctuary ecosystem satisfies both carnivores and raptors, and thrills visitors and volunteers alike.

Sanctuary volunteers and visitors can share dozens of stories like these.

14.5 Volunteers line the Walkway wearing their Sanctuary orange garb
Note the two tigers in the foreground.

It is not an overstatement to say that the operation of the Sanctuary would not be possible without the Sanctuary's dedicated staff and substantial team of volunteers. More than 120 volunteers work in Animal Care and Education and on special projects throughout the year. Volunteers range in age from 17 to 90 and come from all over the Front Range, some a short hop away in Keenesburg and others driving in from as far away as Laramie, Wyoming.

While there are always new volunteers joining the ranks, there are a large number who have been at the Sanctuary for a decade or more, and a few who have been doing so for more than twenty years. Linda Selkurt started volunteering in 1999, "way before," she says, "we were open to the public. We did animal care and maintenance. There was no staff. I really feel privileged to have been here then...We did all the cleaning... We bottle fed the tiger cubs." Jill Johnson and her son visited the first week the Sanctuary opened to the public in 2003. When Romeo, the mountain lion rescued from Montana, "chirped" at Jill she was "absolutely hooked," became a Sanctuary supporter, and later joined the team of volunteers.

To say the volunteer corps is made up of animal lovers is to state the obvious. Jody Golden originally brought her three year old daughter, Amalie, to see the animals; Amalie is fourteen now and Jody has been here ever since, recalling how tiny the place was with the old Welcome Center, no Carnivore Nutrition Center, and only five employees. Kathy Weigle, who started volunteering ten years ago, tells us "I have seen so many animals come so broken and blossom into such confident, secure, and happy animals. Chase, the tiger, is one that always stands out in my mind. I was volunteering the day after he arrived, and he was so upset and angry with the world...I came back the next week and he was already chuffing. He knew he was finally safe. It just warms your heart." Volunteer Nadine first connected with the Sanctuary on a different level. "I was raised in Africa," she tells us. Upon hearing of the Sanctuary's lions, Nadine continues, "I just came out to see and I remember hearing them roar! For me this is home. It's going back to my roots of Africa, of freedom, of home."

Concerned that she might adopt more than a few cats if she volunteered at the local animal shelter, Dee Pierce's husband sagely suggested she check out The Wild Animal Sanctuary, figuring there was little chance she would be bringing home a lion or tiger. "I fell in love with it," Dee remembers, "I started doing everything. Operations. Education. Animal care. But I really love the education...so I took to the Walkway." Jim Anderson has been volunteering in Education since 2015; his whole family has fallen in love with the Sanctuary and Jim's stories about the animals draw clusters of visitors. Chris Humphreys, a wildlife photographer, has been taking photos for the Sanctuary since moving to Colorado from California ten years ago. "I go up on the Walkway," she smiles, "when there are a lot of people...I've got a big 600 lens, so I let everybody look through my lens. They're like, 'Oh my gosh! It's so close!' I love it."

Come rain or shine, wind, or snow, you will find volunteers on the Walkway. You may also find Volunteer Coordinator Abby Matzke up there (although she could as easily be working in the Carnivore Nutrition Center). Abby joined The Wild Animal Sanctuary after working at W.O.L.F. Sanctuary in Bellvue, Colorado. Her energy and enthusiasm are contagious. "Volunteers have always been my favorite people to work with," she remarks, "because they are so dedicated to a cause that they are willing to give their free time...to a sanctuary or a nonprofit that they feel so strongly about. Working with people dedicated to a cause is the most life-changing experience I've had." Abby and the volunteers help visitors become oriented to the large habitats and their residents, answer all manner of questions about the Sanctuary and the captive wildlife crisis, and ensure that the animals are not bothered and are able to go about their daily business.

Adjusting to the enormous scale and scope of prairie habitats that stretch to the horizon can be challenging. Volunteers help visitors appreciate the austere richness of the land and connect to the magnificence, and whereabouts, of the animals. The blur racing across the meadow in the distance is a tiger. A tiny splash of ochre half-a-habitat away is an African lion who has just lifted his head among the tall grasses. Lucy the Syrian brown bear is relaxing against her favorite post. Foxes, Marble and Granite, have curled up for a nap in the shade of a boulder. Jumanji, the black leopard, is hanging out in the tall grass near the road watching for Becca to come by.

Visitors to The Wild Animal Sanctuary are awestruck at seeing hundreds of large carnivores living happily and contentedly in family groups. Some visitors are captivated by the peace of the prairie and the freedom of the animals to roam. Volunteer Joe Spahn talked to a woman who had volunteered at another sanctuary in California. When that sanctuary went out of business the bears were taken in by The Wild Animal Sanctuary. She was overwhelmed by the huge habitats that "her" bears were now occupying, having taken care of them for ten years under less commodious conditions. Dee Pierce met a visitor from Pennsylvania who was so pleased that Ricki had been rescued from the ice cream shop she flew out to see how the black bear was doing – in February. Ricki, of course, was hibernating, something that never occurred to the visitor because Ricki had no place to hibernate in her cage in Pennsylvania.

Visitors ask a lot of questions. Queries coming from the children are especially entertaining. A young schoolboy asked Mark, "How many teeth

14.6 Chase the tiger flies through the snow

does a tiger have?" "Thirty," Mark answered (thanks to Google). "Do you brush the bears' teeth?" asked another. "No," replied Nancy Williams, "but that doesn't mean you shouldn't brush yours!" "Why," visitors ask, "are there tires on top of the poles around the leopard habitat?" The volunteer's response: "To see if eagles would nest there. But they seem to prefer the trees!" "When the lions start roaring," smiles Chris Humphreys, "some visitors ask if it is a recording!" No, we tell them, that is the real deal!

The Sanctuary closes each day at sunset, which is about 8:30 p.m. at the height of summer. All visitors must be off the premises by then. The two to three hours prior to closing, known at the Sanctuary as "Wild Nights," are often the most delightful of the whole day. What is it about the turn from day into night that rouses wild animals? Is it the slowly falling temperatures or nocturnal instincts that flip the switch from big cat enervation to energy and lead them to frolic well into the night?

In any case, the couple of hours leading up to sunset are enchanting. Tigers and lions who have been hidden among the tall grasses or slumbering in underground dens begin to emerge. African lion brothers, Bob and Percy, fly shoulder to shoulder through the spring green grass. Bob leaps and whacks a paw into Percy. Percy whacks back and the big cats race along the fence line toward the Lion House. The starlings and blackbirds gather for one last long flight as the sun arcs behind the mountains. A bobcat asleep in the sun for hours stretches into a deep bow. The foxes play a game of tag, racing around aspens and through long grasses. Wolves begin howling and coyotes yipping. The lions start to roar.

As the sun dips behind the Rocky Mountains, the glow silhouettes peaks that are among the tallest in America. The sky swells and settles on the horizon. High clouds turn from gold to pink and then blaze with crimson. What was peaceful before is now so serene as to seem otherworldly. It is as if the prairie itself heaves a great sigh at the end of another busy day. As we volunteers escort the last visitors of the day back to the Welcome Center, we too find peace and hope in this place like nowhere else on earth.

When we are volunteering on the Walkway, we always thank visitors for coming to see the animals and supporting The Wild Animal Sanctuary. Sometimes they thank us back.

"Thank you," they say, "for volunteering."

"Thank you for being here."

"Thank you for doing this."

"Thank you."

"Thank you."

"Thank you."

Then there are the "thank you's" that stay with you forever. A little boy about five years old shyly approached Dee Pierce with his grandmother.

"Thank you," he said, "for saving them."

"Thank you for saving the animals."

14.7 Kodiak bear Jake seen by visitors from the Walkway

Chapter 15

⁂ ⁂ ⁂ ⁂ ⁂ ⁂ ⁂ ⁂ ⁂ ⁂ ⁂ ⁂ ⁂ ⁂ ⁂ ⁂
⁂ ⁂ ⁂ ⁂ ⁂ ⁂ ⁂ ⁂ ⁂ ⁂ ⁂ ⁂ ⁂ ⁂ ⁂ ⁂

Into the Future: The Wild Animal Refuge

When, in late 2017, the tigers and bears rescued from Joe Exotic's roadside zoo in Oklahoma moved in, the "No Vacancy" sign at The Wild Animal Sanctuary went up. With the build-out of new habitats for the tigers, the Sanctuary's existing prairie acreage had been fully allocated. And, with the number of rescues continuing to build over the years and large rescues becoming more routine, it seemed like the proverbial handwriting was on the wall. There was simply no space left for future rescues; The Wild Animal Sanctuary had run out of room.

From the original 160 acres purchased outside of Keenesburg in 1994, the Sanctuary had grown to 789 acres by acquiring land from surrounding farms. But in 2017 there was no land to be had at a reasonable cost either adjacent to or nearby the existing property. An ever-increasing sea of humanity continued to sprawl along the Front Range, with the urban corridor from Denver to Fort Collins becoming an enormous metroplex. Dirt roads and oceans of wheat were giving way to commuter highways and big box shopping centers. At night, the lights of housing developments in Brighton could be seen cresting the horizon to the west and south of the Sanctuary. Farmers on the plains were selling out to real estate developers at an increasing pace, but residential development was not the only problem. If a developer had not come knocking at the farmer's door, it was likely that an oil company had. New horizontal oil drilling or fracking operations were springing up all around the Sanctuary, resulting in soaring prices for rural acreage. Even if adjacent or nearby farmland did come up for sale, it would be at a price well beyond what it would have cost just a few years earlier.

What had been unthinkable only a decade before had happened more swiftly than anyone anticipated. As Pat Craig lamented in early 2018, "Our becoming virtually landlocked was as sudden and unanticipated as many of our rescues tend to be...it wasn't that long ago when we were sure the

Sanctuary would have many more years filled with options for continuing growth here in Keenesburg. Yet, times change and the accelerated growth we have seen over the past few years has been nothing short of totally shocking." With thousands of large carnivores still in need of rescue, not only in the United States but around the world, the Sanctuary found itself without viable options for giving those rescues their forever home.

The Sanctuary's commitment to large habitats precluded any option to accommodate more animals by carving up the acreage into smaller enclosures. The objective has always been "providing large natural habitats for the animals and protecting them from any undue pressure from humans." Quality of life for a large carnivore means not only nutritious food, fresh water, companionship, and ongoing care, it means being able to *move* across large acreage meadows!

Abandoning the captive wildlife rescue mission was out of the question. The only solution was further expansion and, since there was no contiguous land available at the Sanctuary, that meant finding land elsewhere. But how? And where? No one knew, but in 2017 it was time to figure it out. The hunt for land was on once again. Pat commented, "It was critical that we find a parcel of land that would be logistically viable…it would need to be located where food, staffing and many other resources were close at hand. It also needed to be large enough to serve our mission for decades to come, which meant it would need to be thousands of acres in size, rather than just a few hundred."

15.1 Aerial view of The Wild Animal Refuge

After a few forays into the Colorado mountains and even other states, a solution presented itself in the extreme southeastern part of Colorado. Those who are familiar with the rural landscape stretching to the horizon in all directions near the towns of La Junta, Lamar, and Las Animas on the southeastern plains will envision flat-as-a-pancake fields of grasses, field corn, sweet corn and, of course, the area's famous Rocky Ford melons. But the floodplain of the Arkansas River is not where the Sanctuary found its land. Driving past the sweet corn and melons and angling toward the Oklahoma panhandle on the way to the first Founder's Day in June 2019, we delighted in seeing one of the most remote and pristine areas in the state.

Canyonlands, not cantaloupes, set this region apart. Studded by Piñon pine and juniper woodland, and by great bluffs and red rock outcroppings, the buttes, valleys, and ravines are stunning. Dozens of rugged and rocky draws run like fingers across the rough terrain, sloping sharply down from bony ridges and spurs. Carved out of the hills, the normally dry draws are blessed with ephemeral streams from summer monsoon rains. The dominant topographical landmark is a stunning rock formation long known as "Windsplitter." Aptly named, this massive north facing butte appears from below like the massive hull of a ship slicing its way due north through the canyons. Once bracketed by the northern and southern branches of the Santa Fe Trail, the region had been crisscrossed by cattle drives and settled by ranchers in the nineteenth century. Even today,

15.2 "Windsplitter" at the Refuge

a drive through the region is marked by the metallic rumble of cattle guards and frequent stops to wait for herds to clear the road.

The Clarence Bulkley family was interested in selling a parcel that included 9,004 acres of deeded land and 680 acres of leased land for a total of 9,684 acres. That is an almost mind-boggling amount of acreage, roughly fourteen square miles, five-and-a-half miles long by three-and-a-half miles wide. The nearest town, Springfield is about thirty-seven miles away; La Junta is about sixty miles in the opposite direction. Access to the land is via dirt roads, with the nearest paved road almost twenty miles distant. Most of the land lies in Baca County, one of the least populated and largest acreage counties in Colorado. The remaining twenty-five percent is in Las Animas County, the largest county by land area in the state and one of the most sparsely populated. There is no risk of urban encroachment or commercial development in this distant corner of Colorado.

Not only were the Bulkleys interested in selling the land, the family also was willing to finance the $7 million purchase over five years. Indeed, once they understood the Sanctuary's mission, they became avid supporters of the Refuge. Anticipating the need for additional land purchases as the Sanctuary grew, Pat had started a Wild Open Spaces Fund years before. The Fund was tapped for the $2 million down payment. The remaining money would be obtained from a development program in which donors – who would be known as "Founders" – could "purchase" land on behalf of the animals for $777 an acre. It was a winning combination: enough land for years of rescues, room for immense habitats in a stunning wilderness landscape, a remote location safe from urban sprawl, and a sympathetic landowner willing to help the Sanctuary with financing.

Thus was born The Wild Animal Refuge.

Building the Refuge

This arid and rugged wilderness had almost no road network, no infrastructure, and no electricity or other physical facilities needed for both human and wild animal residents. All would have to be constructed, along with, of course, habitats and fencing, a new Carnivore Nutrition Center (CNC), plus housing and an operations center for animal caregivers. Water, however, would not be a problem. Seven wells and more than thirteen miles of piping had already been installed by the Bulkley family for their livestock and there was ample ground water close to the surface of the land. Although it would take some inventiveness to build fences along the draws and contours of the land, the significant acreage available gave Pat and Casey an opportunity to create enormous naturalistic habitats ranging from thirty-five to more than two hundred acres. Finally, unlike the prairie surrounding Keenesburg, where Sanctuary operations staff has had to construct and maintain ponds, shade structures, and underground dens, as well as plant hundreds of trees, the Refuge property offers abundant shady areas, as well as caves and rock formations where the residents can bed down at night or nap during the day. Pat explains:

Each habitat will have everything from flat grassy areas to hills, bluffs, rock formations, lush forests filled with beautiful pines and natural dens and caves to enjoy. Imagine each cat or wolf being able to explore dense forests that lead to elevated rock outcroppings where they can sit in the warm sun and survey their territory from such a perfect vantage point above! Bears and many of the smaller animals will absolutely love the naturally occurring den sites, and could easily spend years exploring the incredibly diverse topography...This will truly be living as they should, and will be completely different from the horrid lives they left behind.

Construction began in the Spring of 2018 with laying out and grading about thirty miles of access roads inside the property. Remote habitats require broad, well-graded roads for animal caregivers, but also for fire-fighting equipment, rescue trailers and other substantial vehicles that are key to a large carnivore operation. Once the roads were in, the rural electric

15.3 The Wolfhounds and Butchie take a break from construction at the Refuge

association ran power to the location of what would become the new CNC and to the operations complex, located on a high, flat, and level piece of ground toward the southern end of the property.

In the practical and parsimonious spirit of homesteaders who preceded them long ago, the operations team made use of abundant native sandstone in building the new CNC. Enormous stone walls and stacked buttresses serve as a shield against all sorts of weather conditions and provide natural insulation against scorching hot summers and frigidly cold winters. Spray-on concrete lines the inside walls and a corrugated metal roof covers the building.

The views at the operations complex are dramatic in all directions, as is the peace and serenity of this remote piece of the planet. In an ingenious use of recycled and new materials, the operations team designed a cruciform Quonset hut-inspired facility to provide workspace, storage for equipment and supplies, and a dedicated meeting space for Founder's Day events. Four, eighty-foot long ClearSpan structures sit at right angles to each other atop painted cargo shipping containers with an enormous open space in the middle. The operations complex also includes housing for onsite staff and a cell tower. Given that the weather here is as unpredictable as anywhere in Colorado, the team also installed a dedicated weather station.

With some habitats exceeding two hundred acres, the fencing requirements are enormous, as are the construction specifications. As at the Sanctuary, an inner "primary" fence and an outer "perimeter" fence are placed twenty to 100 feet apart. The fences are built with telephone poles set twenty-five feet on center and connected with high-tensile steel.

15.4 Operations Center under construction

15.5 Operations Center completed

15.6 Building habitat fences at the Refuge

The primary fence is strung with eight horizontal strands of electrified "hot" wire to discourage contact by the animals. To put the scale of the operation in perspective: a 300-acre bear habitat at the Refuge requires 2,400 post holes drilled five to seven feet deep to accommodate sixteen to twenty-four inch diameter telephone poles, and 60,000 linear feet of fencing. The habitat fences are built with existing animal migration and movement corridors in mind so as not to interfere with seasonal travel patterns of native species.

By April 2019, the Sanctuary had received its licenses for the Refuge from CPW and the USDA, and accreditation from the GFAS. It was time to start moving in.

Move-In Days Arrive

Given that the Sanctuary has made its name as a home for captive large carnivores, it probably seems curious that a herd of alpacas became the first residents at the Refuge. The fifty Alpacas had arrived at the Sanctuary during a protracted drought about a decade ago. The owners of the alpacas, sadly, were not asking Pat to adopt the fleecy, gentle, and intelligent animals; they were proposing that the Sanctuary feed them to the tigers! Pat immediately agreed to accept the fuzzy-headed herd – but not for tiger food! When the lucky bunch arrived at the Refuge, perhaps thinking they had died and gone to Peru, or even better, heaven, they began exploring the property from top to bottom, returning regularly to their new stone homestead built by the ops team.

15.7 The alpaca herd at the Refuge

The first thirty-five acre big cat habitat was finished in the spring of 2019. The first three big cat residents at the Refuge were an equally unusual trio: two tigers, Budahshay and Bailey, and African lion, Leonardo. While they make an unusual family, all three big cats had lived together as cubs and grown up together into magnificent adult felids. Having been neutered prior to being rescued, Leonardo is the only African lion rescued by the Sanctuary who does not have a mane. Perhaps Budahshay and Bailey see him as just another tiger *sans* stripes!

With additional bear habitats (103 acres for grizzly bears and 243 acres for black bears), the early arrivals have been joined by almost forty new residents, including an assortment of black and grizzly bears, and a number of wolves. The number of bears and size of bear habitats at the Refuge underscore the unique mission of the Sanctuary and opportunity provided by the Refuge. Most sanctuaries, recognizing that constantly roving bears require enormous amounts of space and a varied diet to maintain their health and well-being, have neither the room nor the resources to take care

15.8 Leonardo and Budahshay

of these bruins who can live to be thirty-five to forty years old in captivity. The Refuge meets their requirements perfectly. It is truly heartwarming to think that the grizzly bears, who had spent their lives in 400-square foot enclosures, are now blessed with more than four million square feet of bluffs and rocky outcroppings, Junipers and Piñon pines, wooded valleys, and grassy meadows.

New Refuge residents also include a herd of yaks and some donkeys, a harbinger perhaps of what is to come. The Sanctuary made its reputation creating a high quality home for big cats and bears, and these animals remain its top rescue priority, but the trade in exotic animals hardly stops with them. In addition to the alpacas, camels, llamas, kangaroos and wallabies, donkeys, coati mundi, emus and ostriches, yaks, Patagonian cavies (a large South American rodent), Sulcata tortoises, and more have been rescued by the Sanctuary over the years. Many of these animals have been rehomed to the warmer climates in which they thrive or to other specialized sanctuaries better equipped to care for them.

The massive acreage at The Wild Animal Refuge, however, provides additional opportunities to take in hoofed stock and perhaps other animals that can thrive in the arid, hilly canyons of southeastern Colorado. "The Refuge," Pat observes, "has opened a door...There's so much acreage there that we are not going to use for the big cats and bears that we may as well let them enjoy it. They will have a nice life and will roam free."

The Sanctuary remains dedicated to big carnivores, but if it can crack open the door a little bit and let in a few Tibetan yaks, why not? There's room for just about everybody at the Refuge.

Into the Future

With a commitment to getting the Refuge ready for even more residents, Pat and the core team now shuttle back and forth between the Sanctuary and Refuge. Making sure that the residents are settling in nicely is an important part of the process. Keeping track of large carnivores in huge and, in many cases, heavily wooded habitats requires some innovative techniques. Drones with infrared technology are used to keep tabs on the Refuge residents both day and night. But the animals themselves generally welcome the enclosed four-wheelers driven by animal caregivers, who arrive with breakfast or dinner. Caregivers also visit on random "welfare checks," rewarding the bear or big cat who emerges from beneath a tree or the cool shade of a den with chicken or some other tidbit.

The location in Keenesburg will continue to operate as the main base of operations for The Wild Animal Sanctuary. Its proximity to Front Range cities, ease of access for visitors, continuing and considerable investment in infrastructure and animal services, and Welcome Center and Walkway that serve its educational objectives, make it the premier location for achieving the Sanctuary's multifaceted mission. There are no plans to move the animals at the Sanctuary to the Refuge; however, it is likely that some animals will move periodically from one location to the other depending on their personal needs and circumstances.

The Wild Animal Refuge will not be open to the public, at least for the foreseeable future. An exception is made for Founding Members of the Refuge, who have supported the land acquisition by purchasing an acre or more. During the first Founder's Day weekend, Pat and the Sanctuary team welcomed about nine hundred visitors who drove in for self-guided driving tours, lunch, and a talk by Pat and other members of the Sanctuary team.

The reasons the Refuge is closed to the public are many. First, as those who have attended Founder's Day will attest, the location is exceedingly remote and difficult to access. Second, it takes significant resources to welcome visitors, resources that are currently going to pay off the remaining acreage, as well as to ongoing habitat construction and other major infrastructure projects. But most importantly, given the size of the habitats, the ruggedness of the terrain, and the endless number of hiding places available to its residents, it is unlikely that any visitor would be able to see the rescued animals as they can at Keenesburg. As Pat has remarked, "The forest is so thick, they are almost always hidden somewhere inside… they really do enjoy their new sense of privacy." While Sanctuary visitors are sometimes disappointed about not being able to visit The Wild Animal Refuge, this new "place like nowhere else" perfectly embodies the Sanctuary's mission: the animals always come first.

15.9 Grizzly bear, Miss Montana, emerging from the forest at the Refuge

Chapter 16

Stopping the Captive Wildlife Crisis in Its Tracks

B red in captivity. Born in captivity. Die or be killed in captivity. Over the years, in between those three milestones: bred...born...and dead, we can guarantee that wild animals will suffer. Indeed, as even the few stories we have been able to share with you illustrate, thousands of wild animals living in captivity have been through more than most of us could endure. It is hard to imagine how humans could subject majestic, proud, and sensitive animals to the kind of cruelties we found repeatedly in writing this book. But they do.

The questions are: how can we stop the suffering? How can we stop the captive wildlife crisis in its tracks? The answer can be found in two fundamental solutions. Pass legislation and pass up pets and props.

Legislative Actions: Banning Pets and Props

On the legislative side, there would seem to be three basic options: (1) ban exotic animal ownership, (2) ban exotic animal breeding, and (3) ban public interaction with wild animals.

Loopholes and grandfather clauses in current federal and state laws governing private ownership allow people to sidestep regulations. Plus, the laws are in many cases poorly enforced. The most common sense response would be to ban private ownership completely at the federal level. No loopholes. No grandfather clauses. No licenses. No exemptions. Give the animals up to accredited sanctuaries or suffer the consequences. A sound alternative to the challenges of passing a federal law is to support bans at the state, local or municipal levels. Learn about your state and local captive wildlife ownership laws. At least seventeen states prohibit exotic animal ownership. Why not your state?

As a stop-gap measure to completely ban ownership at the state or federal level, there is always the option of taking on the owners of captive animals one at a time. The petition to free Ricki the ice cream shop bear garnered 200,000 signatures. Dillan, too, was released in part by the power of petitioning. Organizations like Tigers in America, Born Free USA, PETA Foundation's Captive Animal Law Enforcement arm, the Humane Society of the United States, and other similar organizations follow legal violations and sponsor private initiatives.

In the absence of bans on exotic animal ownership, ending all big cat and bear breeding operations would eventually solve the captive wildlife crisis. If we stopped the flow of big cat and bear cubs – the props in most wild animal entertainments – the problem would simply go away in a generation. The existing population of these animals would live out their lives and there would be no more young captive animals in the pipeline.

Banning public interaction with exotic animals also would go a long way to stopping all breeding operations. Cub selfies, petting parties, and swim fests would be illegal. Animal auctions and the black market trade would dry up. The exploitation of big cat and bear cubs would disappear because with human-animal contact barred, there would be no need for young cubs. The tiger mills and other breeding operations would go out of business.

The Big Cat Public Safety Act (as of this writing, awaiting a full vote in the House of Representatives) is a federal law that would get us part way there. While there are exemptions (as always, it seems) for USDA license holders, as well as universities, zoos, sanctuaries (appropriately), and current owners, the Act bans the private ownership of lions, tigers, leopards, cheetahs, jaguars, cougars, or any hybrid of these species (but unfortunately not bears). Given the fact that obtaining a USDA license is a simple task, perhaps the more important restriction in the Act is the ban on direct contact between the public and big cats. With the stroke of a pen, cub petting and selfie operations would be illegal and, without a market for their "products," cub breeders would go out of business.

The problem with any legislation, however, that does not ban *all* ownership of exotic animals is that the breeders and exhibitors will find ways to get around the laws. They always do. Exploiters will switch species or engineer their own. Generic tigers may be protected now, but bears are not. Nor are ligers and tigons. Sadly, those who profit from exotic animals will always find a work-around if the public is willing to pay. Hence the importance of individual initiatives.

Individual Initiatives: Use the Power of Your Purse

There are a couple of things we can all do that would go a long way to stopping the captive wildlife crisis and, given the often glacial speed of legislative processes, may be a lot easier than putting new laws in place. The first is never buy an exotic animal for a pet and the second is stop spending money on wild animal entertainments – especially those that allow human interaction with baby animals.

There would be no need for legislation if people simply stopped buying captive wild animals. Exotic animal ownership is not good for us and it is not good for the animals. Large and small wild carnivores are dangerous, require highly specialized care, and are enormously expensive to keep. They are not supposed to live in the suburbs, in small cages, deprived of interaction with their own kind, and outside of their native habitats. Just because humans have always kept wild animals does not make it right. We will not belabor the point; The Wild Animal Sanctuary's stories of forty years of rescue and rehabilitation speak for themselves.

Even people who would never think of buying a tiger or lion or bear, however, can be drawn into cub petting or cub photo opportunities. Those babies are just so darn cute! Whether a human infant, a kitten or a puppy, a lion or tiger cub, we are irresistibly drawn to big round eyes, a snub nose, silly grins, too-big ears and paws, soft fur, and playful innocence. Humans, it seems, are genetically programmed to treat cuteness with compassion. It is a scientific fact that babies evoke in us the need to cuddle and care for creatures more fragile than ourselves.

Exploiters of, say, tiger cubs know this, and they take full advantage of it. Offering up weeks-old cubs for us to fondle, they are fully aware that many of us will not be able to resist the lure of what so many describe as "the experience of a lifetime!" Perhaps for the tiger fondlers but not for the tiger cub. They are not toys. They are not ours to pass around like furry party favors. Within a few weeks or months the animal will have lived out its useful life as a "cub" and be discarded like yesterday's trash. However much people might love to pet them, to *not* pet them is the better choice.

All we must do to put exotic animal exploiters out of business is to stop paying to play with and take selfies with wild animal babies. It really is quite simple. Think about the power of your purse. We vote with our wallets every time we buy a product or service. Skippy or Jif? Subaru Outback or Ford Escape? Samsung Galaxy or Apple iPhone? When we do not like a product, we avoid it. If we do not want it, we do not buy it.

If we disagree with the purveyor's ethics, we look elsewhere. When we stop buying, sellers listen. When we walk away, businesses die. If we stop spending money on roadside zoos, circuses with wild animal acts, cub pay-to-play and selfie schemes, then captive wild animal entertainments will simply go out of business. It is an easy fix.

If you want to spend your money or your time to see and aid captive wild animals, support a wild animal sanctuary instead.

Support Wild Animal Sanctuaries

As a 501(c)(3) not-for-profit organization, The Wild Animal Sanctuary relies on the donations and contributions of supporters to stay in business – as do all genuine animal sanctuaries. From the rock on the table under which visitors placed a $1 or $10 bill in the early Keenesburg years to the development of more systematic fundraising approaches, the Sanctuary has successfully weathered its share of financial ups and downs. But it has not been easy.

In fact, in 2006 The Wild Animal Sanctuary almost had to close, completely and forever. The curious thing was that the Sanctuary's financial crisis arose from a completely unforeseen source – the generosity of the American people. No one could have predicted that in the early years of the twenty-first century, the world would be slammed by a disaster triple play. The first tragedy came on September 11, 2001. Then the Southeast Asian tsunami hit in 2004. Finally, Hurricane Katrina decimated New Orleans and the Gulf Coast in 2005. Donations to disaster relief efforts for these catastrophes affirm that Americans may be the most generous people on the planet. Donations for 9/11 relief efforts topped $2.5 billion. Those for the tsunami exceeded $1.8 billion. And donations for Hurricane Katrina were an overwhelming $4.2 billion.

With dollars flowing from one disaster to the next, contributions to The Wild Animal Sanctuary dried up. It was not alone; other charitable organizations also felt the pinch as donors shifted their monies to help disaster victims. Ironically, donors may never have considered that reallocating their donations to relief organizations would come at the expense of other not-for-profit organizations. This is not to say that the disaster relief donations were inappropriate but only to say that substituting one charity for another may have unintended, and dire, consequences.

After struggling for years as donations slowed to a trickle, financial reserves fast disappeared, and loans were tapped out, Pat Craig had no choice but to close the Sanctuary and rehome more than 150 wild animals. In August 2006, he wrote to supporters:

> It is with great sorrow and a heavy heart that I write this letter. After nearly 27 years and many hundreds of animals saved, The Wild Animal Sanctuary...is closing its doors...We have tried everything, literally, to keep the Sanctuary operating. We have pursued every idea, every possibility, no matter how remote... Closing is the last thing I ever wanted, and I have done everything I can to avoid it. All I can do now is focus on finding a way to save as many animals as possible...

Pat concluded the letter with an appeal for funding to feed the animals while he was finding new homes for them (which, before grocer food donations, cost upwards of $1 million per year) and then transport them to other sanctuaries across the United States. The letter went out to supporters and then, miraculously, funds started coming in. "Within hours of hearing the Sanctuary was closing, thousands of people began responding by donating and passing on the word to help. Chain emails raced across the country and even overseas...and blogs sprung up everywhere telling our story to the world." Even celebrity Jessica Biel got involved, visiting the Sanctuary and then launching a fundraising campaign through her own charitable network.

Since we are writing this in 2020 and the Sanctuary is now home to more than 500 animals, our story clearly has a happy ending. With additional development tools in place such as an annual Pledge Program the Sanctuary is now on firmer financial footing. But running a Sanctuary for 500-plus carnivores means there is never room for complacency – as demonstrated by the completely unexpected effects of the COVID-19 virus. No one predicted the virus, and no one could have foreseen the impact on the Sanctuary. But when the food hoarding panic hit in March and April, emptying grocery shelves across the country, food donations to the Sanctuary almost came to a halt. Fortunately, with the bears still hibernating and some frozen food reserves on hand, the Sanctuary was able to carry on by purchasing additional meat for the carnivores until gleaning donations picked up again.

The 2006 near-closure and the 2020 food shortage demonstrate the complexity and tenuousness inherent in operating a not-for-profit large carnivore sanctuary as an ongoing business. The enterprise requires the can-do attitude, self-sacrifice, and sophisticated equipment of a first-responder team; the ability to deliver outstanding, high quality care of a major veterinary clinic or animal hospital; the unparalleled animal husbandry and handling capabilities, habitat design, and maintenance of a major public zoo; the sound management capabilities needed to operate a business with a sizeable staff and volunteer corps; and the fundraising savvy and strong donor relationships of a successful not-for-profit organization.

The challenges facing wild animal sanctuaries will only increase in the future as more state and (hopefully) federal laws require the surrendering of wild animal "pets" and "props" used in commercial businesses. Where will those animals find new homes? They cannot be released into the wild for reasons already discussed. Zoos have no room or need for them; they are looking to place their own surplus animals. The only obvious answer is to house them in sanctuaries dedicated to providing them with forever homes.

In sum, wild animal sanctuaries need – and deserve – your support. The key is to make sure that you are helping a true sanctuary and not a "scamtuary," so check out GFAS and consider donating, visiting, and volunteering at one or more of their member organizations.

Chapter 17

Forever Wild, Forever Home

---

*B*e prepared to have your life changed.
  Bold words those. Daring words. Words we heard for the first time on the first day we ever visited The Wild Animal Sanctuary. Yet that is exactly what happened. Our lives changed.

Pat Craig never set out to create the premier large carnivore sanctuary in the world. We never set out to become captive wildlife champions and animal welfare advocates. The day we looked across the broad meadows and enormous habitats that encompass Pat's life's work turned out to be the same day we looked toward what would become an all-encompassing future endeavor – writing this book.

Over the course of four decades Pat has unequivocally changed the captive wildlife paradigm. He was a founder of a wild animal sanctuary at a time when domestic animal welfare dominated public awareness and, as he remembers, "trying to get anyone to listen to the needs or concerns of captive wildlife was darn near impossible." He worked with, and around, antiquated regulations that got his large carnivores out of tiny cages and into green pastures. Slowly, he increased the size and character of habitats so that the animals who came to live at the Sanctuary not only had room to move but to roam, run, play, swim, and explore. Over the years, he has strived to put as much "wild" into his captive wild carnivores as is possible, increasing their autonomy and independence. As a leader in understanding captive large carnivore behavior and a keen observer of animal sentience, communication, and socialization, he fought, and continues to fight, for changes in animal welfare laws.

Pat began answering calls to rescue animals all over the United States and designed and procured specialized trailers and transport cages to get them home to Colorado. When the calls started coming in from well beyond the U.S. borders, Pat learned to wend his way through the

mounds of red tape, becoming an expert at the exotic animal importation process. His dedication to developing nutritionally robust diets coupled with innovative and carefully customized rehabilitation programs have allowed hundreds of abused and suffering animals to become the glorious creatures they were meant to be.

Realizing that the captive wildlife crisis would have no chance of abating without greater public awareness, Pat began focusing efforts on education. Then he literally took public education to new heights by building an elevated walkway that has completely revolutionized how people view wild animals and has proved to be as non-threatening to Sanctuary residents as it is enjoyable to Sanctuary visitors. Pat has never given up on the tripartite mission of rescue, rehabilitation, and education, even when the Sanctuary teetered on the verge of bankruptcy in 2006. When the Sanctuary's 789 acres outside of Keenesburg were fully built out, he negotiated the purchase of 9,684 acres in southeastern Colorado establishing The Wild Animal Refuge. In its enduring commitment to large-acre habitats; bold rescue operations; comprehensive and customized rehabilitation programs; care tailored to the needs of each animal; and sheer size in both acreage and number of animals, The Wild Animal Sanctuary is truly exceptional.

Through Pat's actions and inestimable sense of empathy, we can work toward a captive wildlife code of ethics based on the premise that while the Sanctuary's exotic animals are forever wild, they are also captives and always will be. Humans are responsible for their captivity and the perpetuation of that captivity through extensive breeding, and so, must take responsibility for their care and well-being.

The Five Freedoms, developed in the United Kingdom in the 1960's to promote animal welfare in the agricultural industry, get us only part way there. These freedoms are: (1) freedom from injury and disease; (2) freedom from hunger, thirst, and malnutrition; (3) freedom from thermal or physical distress; (4) freedom to express most "normal" behaviors; (5) freedom from fear. Established more than half a century ago, the Five Freedoms were a start, but given what we now know about animal behavior and emotion, they set the bar too low. Merely surviving is hardly equivalent to thriving; simply living is not the same as enjoying quality of life. With their consistently dour perspective, the Five Freedoms do not begin to reflect the need for captive wild animals to enjoy positive and constructive lives. It is simply not enough to secure freedom *from* cruelty. The noblest aspiration is to ensure that captive wild animals are given the opportunity to experience joy, playfulness, fun, exuberance, curiosity, good cheer, solitude, relaxation, comfort, harmony, friendship, and, yes, happiness.

That is the magic we strive for and what visitors see when they come to The Wild Animal Sanctuary. It not only keeps visitors coming back again and again, it powers the dedication of staff and volunteers. We are drawn to the Sanctuary for so many reasons. Here we discover peace and encounter joy. Seeing the animals heal, we heal as well. Where we saw despair among new rescues, there is now dignity. Where there was infirmity, there is now strength. Where there was defeat, there is now delight. They are survivors and from their resilience and will to live, we too draw courage and resolve. Their lives resonate with our own.

When we look into the eyes of Ronin, catch a glimpse of Jake emerging from his pool, smile at Jumanji swaying on the sky bridge, spot Diego slumbering in the sun, or marvel at any of the hundreds of other animals who call this place their own, we feel with them a deep connection and a profound sense of reciprocity. In the end, we are all members of an incomprehensible, awesome, and fragile Creation, all part of something larger than ourselves, each taking and giving in some measure, spinning along together as passengers on this great big planet Earth.

At The Wild Animal Sanctuary, we take care of grizzly bears and black bears, African lions, jaguars, leopards, mountain lions, tigers, and all manner of other exotic animals – and they take care of us. They rely on us for food and shelter and all the health, well-being, happiness, and love we can possibly give over the course of their natural lives in this, their forever home. We rely on them for hope and joy and, especially, the promise that they will remain forever wild.

For when wildness leaves the world, wonder will soon follow.

E p i l o g u e

:·: :·: :·: :·: :·: :·: :·: :·: :·: :·: :·: :·: :·: :·: :·: :·:
·: ·: ·: ·: ·: ·: ·: ·: ·: ·: ·: ·: ·: ·: ·: ·:

And Texas Makes Three!

As we were wrapping up this book, The Wild Animal Sanctuary boldly expanded once again. With the original Sanctuary in Keenesburg celebrating its fortieth year and the Refuge approaching its two-year anniversary, Pat Craig took another significant step on the journey to rescue and care for captive wild animals.

With the nearly thirty-year tenure of its current administrator ending, the International Exotic Animal Sanctuary (IEAS) in Boyd, Texas, was looking for another organization to assume control of its operations. After carefully researching IEAS, Pat determined that its solid history of rescuing and caring for captive wildlife, its roughly forty acres of heavily wooded habitats, and its dedicated and nurturing staff aligned with the Sanctuary's mission and philosophy. As a result, IEAS, located about thirty miles northwest of Fort Worth, has become The Wild Animal Sanctuary–Texas.

More than seventy new residents, including thirty-six bears, have joined the Sanctuary exotic animal family. Like the Sanctuary, IEAS is one of the few organizations that has traditionally rescued bears. Lions, tigers, wolves, and a variety of other cats and small carnivores round out the total.

Pat and the Sanctuary team are visiting the Texas facility regularly. They have introduced efficiencies related to food donations and handling, animal care, and overall operations and logistics. Although IEAS was giving guided tours prior to COVID-19, without an elevated walkway and with no room to build one, there will be no visitors allowed under Sanctuary management.

The establishment of The Wild Animal Sanctuary–Texas seems a fitting close to this book and noteworthy tribute to Pat Craig and his resolute and passionate staff. Taking responsibility for an entire sanctuary's worth of animals embodies the spirit of The Wild Animal Sanctuary—which from Pat's very first rescue of a tiny jaguar cub named Freckles, has always found a way when there are animals in need.

Notes on Sources and Further Reading

We have utilized many scholarly and academic publications, particularly with respect to the captive wildlife crisis, in researching and writing *Forever Wild, Forever Home.* Here we gratefully acknowledge the chief sources used in this book and offer suggestions for further reading. Every effort has been made to verify the credibility of sources, corroborate information presented, and assess citations and references for credibility and evidence of bias.

The Sanctuary's outstanding website, including its award-winning videos, and its quarterly newsletter, *Sanctuary News,* comprise an invaluable historical treasure trove, detailing rescue and rehabilitation stories, operations and animal care, the work done by staff and volunteers, and the amazing growth of the Sanctuary over the years. Its website, www.wildanimalsanctuary.org, can be accessed for more information and hours of enjoyment provided by photos and videos.

Unless otherwise noted, all quotes by Pat Craig are taken from our conversations with him; his "Letters from the Director" published in *Sanctuary News;* and other articles. Quotes from Sanctuary staff, including Casey Craig, Ryan Clements, Kent Drotar, Becca Miceli, Abby Matzke, Dr. Joyce Thompson, and consulting veterinarian Dr. Felicia Knightly are from conversations, videos, newsletters, or other published sources. Quotes from Sharon Guynup and Steve Winter are from our interview with them and the following sources: Sharon Guynup, photographs by Steve Winter, "The Tigers Next Door," *National Geographic,* December 2019; their interview with Kara Jamie Norton, "The Truth About 'Tiger King' and Cats in Captivity," *Rocky Mountain PBS,* April 6, 2020, pbs.org/went/nature/blog/the-truth-about-tiger-king-and-cats-in-captivity. Quotes from Brittany Peet, Deputy General Counsel for Captive Animal Law Enforcement with the PETA Foundation, are from our interview with her. Quotes from Dr. Peter Emily, Founder, and Susanne Pilla, Board of Directors member, of the Peter Emily International Veterinary Dental Foundation (PEIVDF) were obtained in an interview with them. Jan Creamer's quotes are from the film *Lion Ark.*

1. A Place Like Nowhere Else

There is no shortage of recent articles on Joe Exotic. See Leif Reigstad, "Joe Exotic: A Dark Journey into the World of a Man Gone Wild," *Texas Monthly*, June 2019, www.texasmonthly.com/articles/joe-exotic-a-dark-journey-into-the-world-of-a-man-gone-wild; Karin Brulliard, "The Trouble with Tigers in America," *Washington Post*, July 12, 2019, www.washingtonpost.com/graphics/2019/investigations/captive-tigers-america/; Robert Moor, "American Animals: Joe Exotic Bred Lions, Tigers, Ligers at his Roadside Zoo," *Intelligencer, New York Magazine*, September 3, 2019, nymag.com/intelligencer/2019/09/joe-exotic-and-his-american-animals.html (note, however, that Joe Exotic did not "donate" his tigers to a sanctuary); Sharon Guynup, "'Tiger King' sentenced to 22 years for violence against tigers and people," *National Geographic*, January 24, 2020, www.nationalgeographic.com/ animals/2020/01/tiger-king-joe-exotic-sentenced-22-years-violence-tigers-murder-hire/; Sharon Guynup, "What 'Tiger King' Doesn't Show," *Washington Post*, April 2, 2020; www.washingtonpost.com/opinions /2020/04/02/what-tiger-king-doesnt-show/.

3. Confronting the Captive Wildlife Crisis

Among the many organizations who advocate for the compassionate care of captive wild animals and an end to the captive wildlife crisis are: Animal Defenders International (ADI); the Animal Legal Defense Fund (ALDF); Born Free and its sister organization Born Free USA; Freedom for Animals; and Tigers in America (TIA). Their websites are excellent introductions to the captive wildlife crisis.

The U.S. Fish and Wildlife Service publishes information on the illegal wildlife trade at www.fws.gover/international/travel-and-trade/illegal-wildlife-trade. Traffic, the Wildlife Trade Monitoring Network, is an excellent source of information on the global trade of wild animals and plants. Their publication, "Tigers Among Us" provides a succinct overview of trafficking in tigers and tiger parts and the implications of captive tiger populations on wild tiger conservation, worldwildlife.org/publications/tigers-among-us. Also see Jessica B. Izzo, "PC Pets for a Price: Combating Online and Traditional Wildlife Crime Through International Harmonization and Authoritative Policies,"

34 *Wm. & Mary Envtl. L. & Pol'y Rev.* 965 (2010), scholarship.law. wm.eduwmelpr/vol34/iss3/6. Natasha Daly, photos by Kirsten Luce, "The Wildlife We See, The Suffering We Don't," *National Geographic*, June 2019 provides an overview of wildlife tourism, a significant portion of which involves captive animals.

For an introduction to keeping exotic animals see Lisa Ann Tekancic and Maria Dunbar-Stewart, "The History and Culture of Wildcats in Captivity," *Journal of the WildCat Conservation Legal Aid Society*, Vol. 1 (2009), wcclas.org/wordpress/wpcontent/ uploads /2016/06/History-and-Culture-of-Wildcats-in-Captivity. pdf; Lauren Slater, "Wild Obsession: The Perilous Attraction of Owning Exotic Pets," *National Geographic*, April 2014, www. nationalgeographic.com/magazine/2014/04/exotic-pets/; Adele Young, "Caged Cats: Private Ownership of Lions and Tigers," *Wm. & Mary Envtl. L. & Pol'y Rev*, 535 (2014), scholarship.law. wm.edu/wmelpr/vol38/iss2/8.

Information on tigers, both wild and captive, is plentiful. For a brief overview see "From American Suburbs to Asia's 'Tiger Farms,' The Case Against Keeping Tigers Locked Up," *World Wildlife Magazine*, Winter 2016, www.worldwildlife.org/ magazine/issues/winter-2016/articles/captive-tigers-in-the-us. Ronald Tilson and Philip J. Nyhus, eds., *Tigers of the World: The Science, Politics, and Conservation of Panthera tigris* (London: Elsevier, 2010) is invaluable, particularly with respect to species information and conservation efforts. For an overview of the near extinction of tigers due to trophy hunting, see Sharon Guynup, "A Concise History of Tiger Hunting in India," *National Geographic*, March 10, 2014, blog.nationalgeographic. org/2014/03/10/a-concise-history-of-tiger-hunting-in-india/.

Sources consulted on the history, evolution, and future of zoos include: David Hancocks, *A Different Nature: The Paradoxical World of Zoos and Their Uncertain Future* (Berkeley: University of California Press, 2001); Nigel Rothfels, *Savages and Beasts: The Birth of the Modern Zoo* (Johns Hopkins University Press, 2002); and Vicki Croke, *The Modern Ark: The Story of Zoos: Past, Present and Future* (Scribner, 1997). Devra G. Kleiman, Katerina V. Thompson and Charlotte Kirk Baer, eds., *Wild Mammals in Captivity: Principles and Techniques for Zoo Management*, 2nd edition, (University of Chicago Press, 2012) is a comprehensive volume on the management of captive wild mammals. The Association of Zoos and Aquariums (AZA) website provides information on the organization and its members, as well as conservation and accreditation programs. Public zoo animal populations and acreage were taken from individual zoo websites, accessed June 2020.

A good introduction to stereotypic behaviors in wild animals can be found at Born Free, www.bornfree.org.uk/zoochosis; there also is considerable scholarly research available which tends to be species specific.

Roadside zoos, cub petting and pay-to-play outfits are closely monitored by PETA and HSUS; both organizations are relentless in their pursuit of illegal animal entertainments. General information about Doc Antle's Myrtle Beach Safari can be found on the organization's website; tour specifics mentioned here are located under "Wild Encounters Tour," docantlesdaysafari.com/, accessed August 14, 2020. Tracey McManus, "Dade City's Wild Things closes amid legal fight. Its last 6 tigers removed," *Tampa Bay Times*, April 1, 2020 highlights the closure of a violator of animal welfare laws.

For white tigers specifically, A.K. Roychoudhury and K.S. Sankhala, "Inbreeding in White Tigers," *Indian Academy of Sciences*, Vol. 88, Part I, No. 5, October 1979 provides an authoritative analysis of the inbreeding practices and early mortality rates among the first captive white tigers. The AZA White Paper, "Welfare and Conservation Implications of Intentional Breeding for the Expression of Rare Recessive Alleles," June 2011 highlights the deleterious effects of inbreeding on animal welfare, species diversity, and conservation management.

The major federal laws dealing with captive wildlife are the Lacey Act of 1900, amended by the Captive Wildlife Safety Act in 2007; the Animal Welfare Act of 1966; and the Endangered Species Act of 1973. For an overview of the laws, see Carney Anne Nasser, "Welcome to the Jungle: How Loopholes in the Federal Endangered Species Act and Animal Welfare Act are Feeding a Tiger Crisis in America," 9 Alb. Govt. L. Rev. 194 (2016), albanygovernmentlawreview. org/Articles/. See Chris Heath, "The Crazy True Story of the Zanesville Zoo Escape," *GQ*,

February 6, 2012 for background information on the key event that precipitated captive wildlife law changes in Ohio. The USDA "Pre-License Application Package, Class C Exhibitors" covers the acquisition and costs of an exotic animal license. The USDA is implementing a new licensing rule, effective November 9, 2020; for further information on revised costs and licensing requirements see www.aphis.usda.gov/aphis/ourfocus/animalwelfare/sa_regulated_businesses/new-licensing-rule/new-licensing-rule Both the HSUS and PETA keep tabs on changing state laws.

7. When You've Seen One Rescue…You've Seen One Rescue

Spirit of the Hills Wildlife Sanctuary operations data was obtained from multiple USDA APHIS Inspection Reports dated from September 28, 2016 through October 4, 2016 and financial information was obtained from tax returns and Form 990 documents as compiled on Nonprofit Explorer, https://projects.propublica.org/nonprofits/organizations/460461795, accessed August 15, 2020. The Kodiak bear attack and closing of Silver Springs were widely reported in local area media outlets; see for example "Two Silver Springs bear kill third bear," *Ocala Star Banner*, December 7, 2006, www.ocala.com/article/LK/20061207/News/604247873/OS.

9. Bolivian Lions Come to Colorado

Information about Lion Ark was obtained from the film by the same name; ADI's website, ad-international.org; and other media sources. The Tim Phillips quote about Colo Colo is from Laura Silverman, "Rescue mission of circus lions made into film," *The Telegraph*, November 2014, www.telegraph.co.uk/news/earth/wildlife/11247834/Rescue-mission-of-circus-lions-made-into-film.html.

13. The Doctor – and Dentist – Are In

The information on the Peter Emily International Veterinary Dental Foundation (PEIVDF) was obtained in an interview with Dr. Peter Emily and Susanne Pilla, from their website, peteremilyfoundation.org/wild-animal-sanctuary-co/, and from Sanctuary newsletters.

17. Forever Wild, Forever Home

The language of the five freedoms can differ slightly depending on the source. The list herein was taken from Kleiman, et.al., *Wild Mammals in Captivity*. Marc Bekoff's books are excellent and enjoyable introductions to animal sentience and the moral imperative for our ethical treatment of them. See for example, Marc Bekoff, *The Animal Manifesto: Six Reasons for Expanding our Compassion Footprint* (New World Library, 2010) and Marc Bekoff, *The Emotional Lives of Animals* (New World Library, 2007).

CPSIA information can be obtained
at www.ICGtesting.com
Printed in the USA
BVHW061918041220
594493BV00005B/9

9 781662 903205